A Day with the Prophet ﷺ

By
Shaykh Muftī Saiful Islām

JKN Publications

First Published in October 2020

ISBN 978-1-909114-63-0

British Library Cataloguing in Publication Data
A catalogue record for this book is available from the British Library.

Publisher's Note:

Every care and attention has been put into the production of this book. If however, you find any errors they are our own, for which we seek Allāh's ﷻ forgiveness and the reader's pardon.

Published by:

JKN Publications
118 Manningham Lane
Bradford
West Yorkshire
BD8 7JF
United Kingdom

t: +44 (0) 1274 308 456 | w: www.jkn.org.uk | e: info@jkn.org.uk

Book Title: A Day with the Prophet ﷺ

Author: Shaykh Mufti Saiful Islām

Printed by Mega Printing in Turkey

"In the Name of Allāh, the Most Beneficent,
the Most Merciful"

Contents

Preface

In the Name of Allāh, the Most Gracious, the Most Merciful

The appearance of the Messenger of Allāh 🝿 was one of the greatest blessings that Allāh 🝿 bestowed upon mankind. Not only did our beloved Prophet 🝿 achieve the highest success in his mission but also left behind a glorious legacy to benefit mankind. Over fourteen hundred years have passed and yet his influence still shines over the modern world impacting the lives of millions of people positively. Every detailed narrative of his noble sayings, actions, biography, habits, physical description and character are preserved until today through an uninterrupted chain of transmission.

Yet unfortunately, the number of Muslims appreciating his legacy and following in his footsteps are very little in comparison with the vast number of Muslims spread throughout the world. Due to our shortcomings, many of us are oblivious of many of his precious Sunnats related to his noble daily habits. Allāh 🝿 has declared in the holy Qur'ān of our beloved Prophet 🝿 being an exemplary role model for us all. He states, **Verily for you there is in the Messenger of Allāh an excellent example. (33: 21).**

Allāh 🝿 our Creator and Benefactor has stamped a seal of approval in this verse of his life and teachings setting an excellent standard for us to adopt. Hence, there isn't a single facet in a human being's life the Messenger of Allāh 🝿 has left out for us.

With this frame of mind, this treatise before you is a collection of the daily Prophetic Sunnats - practices and habits - a guide for us all to follow. The objective behind this book is to instil the love for the Prophet ﷺ by encouraging our readers to implement his Sunnats into their daily lives. The daily Sunnats range from worship to general social and personal etiquettes and conduct. Each habit relative to a specific Sunnat is referenced from a hadīth. On the face of it, it may appear overwhelming but I can assure you that once you start to slowly implement them, then overtime they gradually become your secondary nature. Each Sunnat is never difficult to adopt for a true believer.

Amongst many of the JKN publications I have read from cover to cover whilst editing, I must confess that this book was very different and life changing for me. During the editing process, I discovered so much more when cross checking for the references to ensure they were sound and established. I only realised how little we know about the Prophetic Sunnats. I am truly grateful to Shaykh Mufti Saiful Islām for compiling this to benefit us all. May Allāh ﷻ preserve him, reward all those brothers and sister who contributed their efforts in facilitating this noble project, grant acceptance to it and most importantly, make this as a means of earning our beloved Prophet's ﷺ love and companionship in the Hereafter, Āmīn.

(*Mufti*) *Abdul Waheed*
JKN Institute & Fatawa Department
Dhul-Hijjah 1441 AH / August 2020

Introduction

نَحْمَدُهُ وَ نُصَلِّى عَلَى رَسُوْلِهِ الْكَرِيْمِ وَ عَلَى اٰلِهٖ وَ اَصْحَابِهٖ اَجْمَعِيْنَ اَمَّا بَعْدُ

All praises truly belong to Allāh ﷻ, the Lord of the worlds, Who we can never praise, thank or worship the way He truly deserves. May Allāh's ﷻ infinite blessings be upon our beloved Rasūl and Master, Muhammad ﷺ. May countless blessings also be upon his noble Companions ﵁, pure family and blessed Ummah, until the end of times. Āmīn.

For Muslims, the holy Qur'ān and the sunnah of Rasūlullāh ﷺ govern our lives. Both are crucial and complement each other. We are extremely fortunate in that our Messenger ﷺ was a true embodiment of the Qur'ān, so by following him, in essence, we are following the injunctions of the holy Qur'ān.

However, it is an unfortunate truth that the word 'sunnah' doesn't have the desired affect it ought to have on the hearts of Muslims today. Many Muslims have accumulated so much sins and wrongdoings throughout the years that our hearts have become infected with spiritual illnesses and maladies. It is for this reason that unfortunately hearing the word 'sunnah', doesn't hold much significance to us as it should do like it did with the Sahābah ﵁ and the Tābi'īn ﵂.

Following the sunnah rigorously is a means of gaining closeness and friendship with Allāh ﷻ. Subhān'Allāh, if we were to look at the Sahābah ؓ and the Salaf us-Sālihīn ؒ, we'd notice many qualities they all shared one of them namely; their love for the sunnah. They held the sunnah of Rasūlullāh ﷺ in high esteem such that it was either the sunnah, or no other way. You can therefore understand, how Allāh ﷻ granted them such acceptance and favours.

In Sūrah Yūnus, Allāh ﷻ states:

$$ ۞ أَلَا إِنَّ أَوْلِيَآءَ اللّٰهِ لَا خَوْفٌ عَلَيْهِمْ وَلَا هُمْ يَحْزَنُونَ $$

Unquestionably, (for) the friends of Allāh there will be no fear concerning them, nor will they grieve. (10:62)

Eagerly following the sunnah of Rasūlullāh ﷺ is one way of working towards attaining the high rank of becoming amongst the awliyā' (friends) of Allāh ﷻ. This refers to the sunnah in all aspects of life.

A unique and distinguishing aspect of Islām in comparison to other religions is the vast knowledge and guidance given pertaining to all aspects of human life. In the sunnah, we are shown how to behave in all spheres of life; from the most obvious behaviours such as salāh, to even the most intimate of actions such as visiting the lavatory. Islām is such a comprehensive religion; a complete way of life.

Alhamdulillāh, in this book, my honourable ustādh and shaykh - Mufti Saiful Islām Sāhib - has compiled various sunnats of Rasūlullāh ﷺ pertaining to different aspects of life. It is hoped that this book will be taught within the curriculums of madāris worldwide as an attempt to instil students with a firm understanding and knowledge regarding the sunnah. This is of vital importance during one's youth so that good habits can develop and continue throughout adulthood.

May Allāh ﷻ accept the constant efforts of our esteemed Mufti Sāhib, who has dedicated his life for the khidmat of dīn. May Allāh ﷻ accept all the noble projects Mufti Sāhib is involved in, namely, our blessed madrasah, Jāmiʿah Khātamun Nabiyeen; its teachers, students, supporters and all those who have a love towards it. May Allāh ﷻ also accept my extremely minor and flawed efforts in this publication - an opportunity I am truly grateful for, despite being completely underserving of. Āmīn, yā Rabbal-ʿĀlamīn.

Dhākirah ʿAlī
Student of JKN
Shawwāl 1441 AH / June 2020

Sunnats upon Awakening

1. Upon awakening, mildly rub both the palms on the face and eyes so that the sleep disappears. *(Bukhārī)*

2. Thereafter, recite the du'ā:

اَلْحَمْدُ لِلّٰهِ الَّذِيْ أَحْيَانَا بَعْدَ مَا أَمَاتَنَا وَإِلَيْهِ النُّشُوْرُ

Alhamdu lillāhil-ladhī ahyānā ba'da mā amātanā, wa ilayhin nushūr.

All praises are due to Allāh Who has given us life after taking it away, and to Whom we shall be resurrected. (Bukhārī)

3. Perform miswāk. *(Ahmad, Abū Dāwūd)*

4. Wash both hands up to the wrists thrice before dipping it into a vessel for using water. *(Muslim)*

5. To perform wudhū. *(Bukhārī)*

6. To awaken other members of the family for the Fajr Salāh. *(Abū Dāwūd)*

Sunnats of Istinjā (Toilet)

Istinjā is the cleaning of the private parts after passing urine and stool by means of toilet paper and water.

1. Whilst going to the toilet, one should wear sandals and cover the head. *(Bayhaqi)*

2. Before entering the toilet, the following du'ā should be read:

اَللّٰهُمَّ إِنِّيْ أَعُوْذُ بِكَ مِنَ الْخُبُثِ وَالْخَبَائِثِ

Allāhumma innī a'ūdhu bika minal khubuthi wal khabā'ith.

O Allāh! I seek protection in You from the male and female devil.
(Bukhārī)

3. To enter the toilet with the left foot. *(Ibn Mājah)*

4. If toilets are not available, then one should ensure that one goes so far that none can see him i.e. a place of privacy. *(Muslim, Nasa'i)*

5. One should not relieve oneself at such places where people generally rest or use for other purposes e.g. pathways, roads, under a tree or a pond. *(Abū Dāwūd)*

6. Not to urinate in the bath or shower. *(Ibn Mājah)*

7. One should sit and urinate so that the urine does not splash onto him. It is wrong to stand and urinate. *(Tirmidhī)*

8. To lower oneself as much as possible before undressing for istinjā. *(Abū Dāwūd)*

9. Not to take any Islamic item in the toilet e.g. ring or locket that has the name of Allāh ☙, the Prophet ☙ or any verse of the holy Qur'ān. *(Abū Dāwūd)*

10. One should not face nor show one's back towards the qiblah whilst relieving oneself. *(Bukhārī)*

11. One should not talk whilst in the toilet except in emergency. *(Ibn Mājah)*

12. Whilst performing istinjā, one should use the left hand and avoid using the right hand. *(Bukhārī)*

13. Istinjā should first be made with earth (or toilet paper) and then with water. *(Abū Dāwūd)*

14. When exiting the toilet, one should step out with the right foot. *(Tirmidhī)*

15. Once outside the toilet, the following du'ā should be read:

$$\text{غُفْرَانَكَ اَلْحَمْدُ لِلّٰهِ الَّذِيْ أَذْهَبَ عَنِّي الْأَذٰى وَعَافَانِيْ}$$

Ghufrānaka alhamdulillāhil-ladhī adhaba 'annil adhā wa 'āfānī.

O Allāh! I seek Your pardon. All praises are due to Allāh Who has taken away from me discomfort and granted me relief. (Abū Dāwūd, Ibn Mājah)

Sunnats of Ghusl (Bath)

1. One should perform ghusl in privacy. *(Bukhārī)*
2. To wash both the hands up to the wrists at the beginning of ghusl. *(Bukhārī)*
3. To wash the private parts. *(Bukhārī)*
4. To wash any other impurities found on the body. *(Bukhārī)*
5. One should perform the complete wudhū. If used water does not flow off, then to delay the washing of the feet till the end. *(Bukhārī)*
6. Not to use excessive water. *(Ibn Mājah)*
7. To pour water over the head, then the right shoulder and then the left shoulder three times. *(Bukhārī)*
8. One should ensure that water reaches every part of the body. *(Abū Dāwūd)*
9. To pour water over the entire body three times. *(Bukhārī)*
10. To clean the body by rubbing it. *(Bukhārī)*
11. After the ghusl, to wipe the body dry. *(Bukhārī)*

Note: If a woman's hair is plaited, then she is excused from loosening her plaited hair, but it is compulsory for her to wet the base of every hair. If she fails to do so, her ghusl will not be valid.

Sunnats of Wudhū

1. To perform wudhū at home and then go for salāh. *(Bukhārī)*
2. To remain in the state of wudhū at all times. *(Ibn Mājah)*
3. Not to waste water during wudhū. *(Ibn Mājah)*
4. To make an intention. One should make the intention to get rid of hadas asghar (in need of wudhū). *(Bukhārī)*
5. To recite Bismillāh. *(Tirmidhī)*
6. To start from the right-hand side. *(Ibn Mājah)*
7. To wash both hands up to the wrists three times. *(Bukhārī)*
8. Brushing the teeth with miswāk. *(Bukhārī, Muwatta' Mālik)*
9. To recite the du'ā whilst performing wudhū:

اَللّٰهُمَّ اغْفِرْ لِيْ ذَنْبِيْ وَوَسِّعْ لِيْ فِيْ دَارِيْ وَبَارِكْ لِيْ فِيْ رِزْقِيْ

Allāhumagh fir lī dhambī wa wassi' lī fī dārī wa bārik lī fī rizqī.

O Allāh! Forgive my sins, grant me expansion in my home and bless my livelihood. (Tirmidhī)

10. Gargling three times. *(Bukhārī)*
11. Pouring water into the nostrils three times. *(Bukhārī)*
12. Washing of each part three times. *(Abū Dāwūd)*
13. Khilāl (passing of wet fingers) of the beard. *(Abū Dāwūd)*
14. Khilāl of the fingers and toes. *(Ahmad, Abū Dāwūd)*
15. Masah of the whole head once. *(Bukhārī)*
16. Masah of the ears. *(Nasa'i)*

17. To perform wudhū systematically. *(Bukhārī)*
18. Not to wash any part more than three times. *(Abū Dāwūd)*
19. To recite the following du‘ā after wudhū:

أَشْهَدُ أَنْ لَّا إِلٰهَ إِلَّا اللهُ وَحْدَهُ لَا شَرِيْكَ لَهُ وَأَشْهَدُ أَنَّ مُحَمَّدًا عَبْدُهُ وَرَسُوْلُهُ اَللّٰهُمَّ اجْعَلْنِيْ مِنَ التَّوَّابِيْنَ وَاجْعَلْنِيْ مِنَ الْمُتَطَهِّرِيْنَ

Ash hadu al-lā ilāha illallāhu wahdahū lā sharīka lahū, wa ash hadu anna
Muhammadan ‘abduhū wa rasūluhū, Allāhummaj ‘alnī minat-tawwābīna,
waj ‘alnī minal muta-tahhirīn.

*I bear witness that there is none worthy of worship but Allāh, and I bear
witness that Muhammad is His Servant and Messenger. O Allāh! Make
me of the repenters and among those who love to be clean. (Tirmidhī)*

20. To use a towel for drying. *(Tirmidhī)*
21. To perform two rak‘āt of tahiyyatul-wudhū after the wudhū
    (except at the makrūh and forbidden times of salāh).

Sunnats Regarding Miswāk

1. Whilst performing wudhū, to clean the teeth with miswāk. *(Ahmad)*

Times when Miswāk is Sunnat
1. Before performing salāh. *(Bukhārī)*
2. After entering one's home. *(Muslim)*
3. Upon awakening. *(Bukhārī, Muslim)*

Recommended Times for the Usage of Miswāk
1. For the recitation of the holy Qur'ān.
2. For the studying of ahādīth.
3. When the mouth emits an odour.
4. For teaching the dīn.
5. For doing dhikrullāh.
6. Before attending a gathering.
7. When experiencing hunger or thirst.
8. After the signs of death are clear.
9. Before and after meals.
10. Before sleeping whether during the day or night.

Note: It is recommended that a miswāk is no longer than a hand span i.e. the maximum distance between the tip of the thumb and little finger, and it should not be thicker than a finger's breadth. *(al-Bahrur-Rā'iq)*

A miswāk should be held in such a manner that the small finger and thumb is below the miswāk and the remaining fingers on its upper side.

A person should start from the right and use a side motion rather than up and down, as the latter method may harm the gums.

Some Benefits of Miswāk

1. Miswāk removes bad smell and creates fragrance in the mouth.
2. Miswāk sharpens the memory.
3. Miswāk is a cure for illnesses.
4. Miswāk strengthens the gums and prevents tooth decay.
5. Miswāk is a cure for headaches.
6. Miswāk strengthens the eyesight.
7. Miswāk assists in digestion.
8. It creates nūr (light) on the face of the one who continuously uses it.
9. The reward of salāh is multiplied seventy times if miswāk is used before it.
10. The greatest benefit of using miswāk is gaining the pleasure of Allāh ﷻ.
11. It will inshā'Allāh remind the person of the kalimah shahādah before he dies.

Sunnats of Adhān

1. To call out the adhān *only* for the pleasure of Allāh 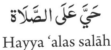. (*Tirmidhī*)
2. For the mu'addhin to be pious. (*Abū Dāwūd*)
3. For the mu'addhin to have a loud voice. (*Abū Dāwūd*)
4. To call out the adhān at its appointed time. (*Musnad ash-Shāfi ʿī*)
5. To call out the adhān in the state of wudhū. (*Tirmidhī*)
6. To call out the adhān from an elevated place. (*Abū Dāwūd*)
7. To face the qiblah when calling out the adhān. (*Abū Dāwūd*)
8. To call out the adhān in the standing posture. (*Abū Dāwūd*)
9. To insert the fingers in the ears whilst calling out the adhān. (*Tirmidhī*)
10. To call out the adhān with the correct words mentioned in the ahādīth. (*Abū Dāwūd*)
11. Not to make haste in calling out the adhān. (*Tirmidhī*)
12. To turn the face towards the right when saying:

حَيَّ عَلَى الصَّلَاة

Hayya ʿalas salāh
Come to salāh

and to the left when saying:

حَيَّ عَلَى الْفَلَاح

Hayya ʿalal falāh
Come to success.

13.   To say:

اَلصَّلَاةُ خَيْرٌ مِّنَ النَّوْمِ

As-salātu khayrum minan-nawm

Salāh is better than sleep

twice after "Hayya 'alal falāh" in the adhān of Fajr. *(Abū Dāwūd)*

14.   To recite the following du'ā after listening to the adhān:

أَشْهَدُ أَنْ لَّا إِلٰهَ إِلَّا اللهُ وَحْدَهٗ لَا شَرِيْكَ لَهٗ وَأَنَّ مُحَمَّدًا عَبْدُهٗ وَرَسُوْلُهٗ رَضِيْتُ بِاللهِ رَبًّا وَّبِمُحَمَّدٍ رَسُوْلًا وَّبِالْإِسْلَامِ دِيْنًا

Ash hadu al-lā ilāha illallāhu wahdahū lā sharīka lahū, wa anna
Muhammadan 'abduhū wa rasūluhū, radītu billāhi rabban wa bi
Muhammadin rasūlan wa bil-islāmi dīnan.

*I bear witness that there is none worthy of worship except Allāh Alone,
with no partner or associate, and that Muhammad is His slave and
Messenger; I am content with Allāh as my Lord, Islām as my religion and
Muhammad as my Messenger.*

A person who recites this du'ā will get all his past sins forgiven.
(Muslim, Nasa'i)

15. To recite the following du‘ā at the time of the adhān of Maghrib:

اَللّٰهُمَّ إِنَّ هٰذَا إِقْبَالُ لَيْلِكَ وَإِدْبَارُ نَهَارِكَ وَأَصْوَاتُ دُعَاتِكَ فَاغْفِرْ لِي

Allāhumma inna hādhā iqbālu laylika, wa idbāru nahārika, wa aswātu du‘ātika, faghfir lī.

O Allāh, this is the time when Your night comes in, Your day retires and the voices of Your callers are heard, so forgive me. (Abū Dāwūd)

16. To reply to the adhān. *(Muslim)*

Note: Repeating the words of adhān and iqāmah is known as ijābah (or replying). Ijābah for both adhān and iqāmah is mustahab (recommended). Those hearing the adhān and iqāmah should repeat the words of adhān and iqāmah as the mu’addhin says. However, after hearing "Hayya ‘alas salāh" and "Hayya ‘alal falāh", one should say "Lā hawla wa lā quwwata illā billāh". *(Muslim)*

17. To recite durūd sharīf after the adhān. *(Muslim)*
18. After the recital of durūd sharīf, to recite the following du‘ā:

اَللّٰهُمَّ رَبَّ هٰذِهِ الدَّعْوَةِ التَّامَّةِ وَالصَّلَاةِ الْقَائِمَةِ أٰتِ مُحَمَّدًا الْوَسِيلَةَ وَالْفَضِيلَةَ وَابْعَثْهُ مَقَامًا مَّحْمُودًا الَّذِي وَعَدْتَهُ

Allāhumma Rabba hādhi hid-da' watit tāmma, was salātil qā'imah, āti Muhammada nil wasīlata wal fadīlata, wab 'ath hu maqāmam mahmūda nil ladhī wa 'attah.

O Allāh, Lord of this perfect call and established salāh, grant Muhammad a place near to You, an excellence and exalted degree and raise him to the praiseworthy station that You have promised him.

Whoever recites this du'ā will gain the intercession of the holy Prophet ﷺ on the Day of Judgement. *(Bukhārī)*

19. Not to leave the masjid without a valid excuse after the adhān is called. *(Abū Dāwūd)*
20. To supplicate between the adhān and iqāmah. *(Abū Dāwūd)*

Du'ās are readily accepted between the adhān and iqāmah.

21. For the mu'addhin to call out the iqāmah. *(Abū Dāwūd)*
22. Iqāmah, in comparison to adhān should be called out quickly. *(Tirmidhī)*
23. To reply to the iqāmah and after the mu'addhin says, قَدْ قَامَتِ الصَّلَاةُ (qad qāmatis salāh), one should say in reply:

Aqāmahallāhu wa adāmahā.
May Allāh establish it and keep it forever. (Abū Dāwūd)

Sunnats of the Masjid

1. To perform wudhū at home and then proceed to the masjid. *(Bukhārī)*
2. To enter with the right foot. *(Bukhārī)*
3. When entering the masjid, a person should send durūd upon the holy Prophet 🕌 and thereafter recite the following duʿā:

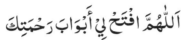

Allāhummaf tah lī abwāba rahmatika.

O Allāh, open for me the doors of Your mercy. (Muslim, Abū Dāwūd)

Any person who recites this duʿā after entering the masjid, then Shaytān says, "He (the reciter) has safeguarded himself from me for the entire day." *(Abū Dāwūd)*

4. To proceed to the masjid with the intention of seeking or teaching knowledge. *(Ibn Mājah)*
5. To perform tahiyyatul-masjid. *(Bukhārī)*
6. Not to raise ones voice in the masjid or engage in futile talk. *(Ibn Mājah)*
7. To recite durūd sharīf when leaving the masjid. *(Abū Dāwūd)*
8. When leaving the masjid, exit with the left foot. *(Bukhārī)*

9. Recite the following du‘ā when leaving the masjid:

اَللّٰهُمَّ إِنِّيْ أَسْأَلُكَ مِنْ فَضْلِكَ

Allāhumma innī as aluka min fadlika.

O Allāh, I ask of You, Your favour. (Muslim, Abū Dāwūd)

10. To make an intention for attending the next salāh when leaving the masjid. *(Bukhārī)*

11. A person whose heart is attached to the masjid will be under the shade of Allāh's  throne when there will be no shade except His shade. *(Bukhārī)*

Sunnats of Salāh

1. To stand upright at the time of takbīr-tahrīmah (opening takbīr) without bowing the head. *(Bukhārī)*
2. To spread the feet the distance equal to four fingers when standing. *(Nasa'i)*
3. Men to raise the hands for the opening takbīr to the level of the ears *(Abū Dāwūd)*. A woman will raise her hands to the level of her shoulder. *(Dār Qutnī)*
4. While raising the hands for takbīr, one should keep the fingers of both hands raised, with the fingers naturally apart. *(Tirmidhī)*
5. To keep the palms of the hands towards the qiblah. *(Marāqil-Falāh)*
6. The muqtadi's (follower of the imām) takbīr-tahrīmah will be together with the imām. *(Bukhārī, Muslim)*
7. To place the right hand over the left hand under the navel. *(Muslim, Dār Qutnī)*

The method of this is to place the inside of the right hand over the top part of the left hand, forming a circle with the little finger and thumb around the wrist.

A female should place her hands on her chest without a formation of a circle with her hands.

8. To read thanā (in the first rak'āt only). *(Abū Dāwūd)*

9. To read ta'awwudh (A'ūdhu billāhi minash-Shaytānir rajīm) only in the first rak'āt. *(Hidāyah)*

10. To recite tasmiyah (Bismillāh hir-Rahmānir-Rahīm) (in every rak'āt) before Sūrah Fātihah. *(Tirmidhī)*

11. To say "Āmīn" after the recitation of Sūrah Fātihah. *(Bukhārī)*

12. To recite thanā, ta'awwudh, tasmiyah and āmīn silently. *(Majma uz-Zawā'id, I'lā us Sunan)*

13. To recite from Sūrah al-Hujurāt to Sūrah al-Burūj in Fajr and Zuhr Salāh. To recite from Sūrah al-Burūj to Sūrah al-Bayyinah in 'Asr and 'Ishā Salāh. For Maghrib Salāh, to recite from Sūrah Bayyinah to the end. *(Nasa'i, Tirmidhī, Musannaf Abdur Razzāq)*

This will be applicable if one is a muqīm (resident). If one is a traveller, then he may recite any sūrah he wishes.

14. To say takbīr (Allāhu Akbar) whilst going into ruk'ū. *(Bukhārī)*

15. To grasp the knees in ruk'ū with open fingers. *(Tirmidhī)*

A female will keep her fingers together. *(Nūrul Iydhah)*

16. In ruk'ū, the male should keep the back and head on the same level and stretch the hands straight, keeping them away from the ribs. The calves should also be straight. *(Ibn Mājah)*

A female should bend only to the extent that her hands reach the knees. *(Raddul-Muhtār)*

17. To recite "Subhāna Rabbiyal 'Azīm" at least three times in ruk'ū. *(Abū Dāwūd)*

18. Whilst coming up from ruk'ū, the imām should say "Sami' Allāhu liman hamidah", followed by "Rabbanā lakal hamd" by the muqtadī (the one who follows the imām). The munfarid (i.e. the one who reads salāh alone) should say both. *(Bukhārī)*

19. To say "Allāhu Akbar" whilst going into sajdah. *(Muslim)*

20. Whilst going into sajdah, first place the knees, then the hands, then the nose and then the forehead on the ground. Additionally, it is sunnah to do the opposite when rising from sajdah i.e. raise the face, then the hands and lastly, the knees. *(Abū Dāwūd)*

21. To perform the sajdah between the palms. *(Muslim)*

22. To keep the fingers together in sajdah, facing the qiblah and the toes should also be turned towards the qiblah. *(Bukhārī)*

23. A male should keep his thighs away from his stomach, forearms off the ground, and upper arms away from ribs i.e. sajdah should be made with the body not pressed on the ground. *(Abū Dāwūd)*

A female should connect her abdomen with her thighs. i.e. a female's sajdah should be pressed on the ground. *(Bayhaqi, Sunan ul-Kubrā)*

24. In sajdah to read "Subhāna Rabbiyal-A'lā" at least three times. *(Abū Dāwūd)*

25. Whilst raising the head from sajdah to say, "Allāhu Akbar." *(Muslim)*

26. In qaidah and jalsah (the sitting between the two sajdahs), to place the left foot horizontally on the ground and to sit on it and keep the right foot vertical so that the toes are facing the qiblah. Also, both palms should be placed on the thighs with the fingers facing towards the qiblah. *(Nasa'i)*

A female should adopt the tawarruk style of sitting which is one's posterior (buttocks) on the ground and the left foot on its side, emerging from under the right which is vertical. *(Nūrul Iydhah)*

27. To say "Allāhu Akbar" and make the second sajdah. *(Muslim)*
28. To raise the index finger of the right hand as one says, "Ash hadu Allāh ilāha" and to lower it at "illallāh". *(Abū Dāwūd)*
29. To recite Sūrah Fātihah in the third and fourth rak'āt of only the fardh salāh. *(Bukhārī)*
30. To recite durūd sharīf in the last qaidah (sitting) after tashahhud. *(Bukhārī)*
31. To recite du'ā after the durūd sharīf. *(Tirmidhī)*
32. To turn the face to the right and left whilst making salām. *(Bukhārī)*

Sunnats after the Completion of Salāh

1. On completing the salāh, one should recite istighfār thrice i.e. "astaghfirullāh" and thereafter say:

اَللّٰهُمَّ أَنْتَ السَّلَامُ وَمِنْكَ السَّلَامُ تَبَارَكْتَ يَا ذَا الْجَلَالِ وَالْإِكْرَامِ

Allāhumma Antas Salāmu wa minkas salāmu tabārakta yā Dhal Jalāli wal Ikrām.

O Allāh, You are as-Salām (One free from every defect), and as-salām (safety from every evil) is (sought) from You. Blessed are You, O Possessor of glory and honour. (Muslim)

2. Thereafter, recite the Tasbīh Fātimi:

Thirty-three times, 'Subhān'Allāh'
Thirty-three times, 'Alhamdulillāh'
Thirty-four times, 'Allāhu Akbar' *(Tirmidhī)*

3. Also recite the fourth kalimah with the following du'ā:

لَا إِلٰهَ إِلَّا اللهُ وَحْدَهُ لَا شَرِيْكَ لَهُ لَهُ الْمُلْكُ وَلَهُ الْحَمْدُ وَهُوَ عَلَى كُلِّ شَيْءٍ قَدِيْرٌ اَللّٰهُمَّ لَا مَانِعَ لِمَا أَعْطَيْتَ وَلَا مُعْطِيَ لِمَا مَنَعْتَ وَلَا يَنْفَعُ ذَا الْجَدِّ مِنْكَ الْجَدُّ

Lā ilāha illallāhu waḥdahū lā sharīka lahū, lahul mulku, wa lahul ḥamdu, wa Huwa 'alā kulli shay'in Qadīr. Allāhumma lā māni'a limā a'ṭayta, wa lā mu'ṭiya limā mana'ta, wa lā yanfa'u dhal jaddi minkal jaddu.

There is nothing which deserves to be worshipped except Allāh Alone Who has no partner; to Him belongs the kingdom, to Him praise is due, and He has power over everything. O Allāh! There is no one that can prevent You from what You give, and none can give that which You prevent and the wealth of the rich will be of no avail to them against You.
(Bukhārī, Muslim)

4.   To recite Āyatul Kursī.

Sayyidunā Abū Umāmah ﷺ relates that the Messenger of Allāh ﷺ said, "Whoever recites Āyatul Kursī after every fardh salāh, then nothing shall prevent him from entering Paradise except death. *(Nasa'i)*

Comprehensive Du'ās

Some comprehensive du'ās from the Qur'ān:

رَبَّنَا تَقَبَّلْ مِنَّا إِنَّكَ أَنْتَ السَّمِيعُ الْعَلِيمُ ۞

Rabbanā taqabbal minnā innaka Antas Samī'ul 'Alīm.

Our Lord! Accept (this worship) from us; You are the All-Hearing, the All-Knowing. (2:127)

رَبَّنَا آتِنَا فِي الدُّنْيَا حَسَنَةً وَّفِي الْأَخِرَةِ حَسَنَةً وَّقِنَا عَذَابَ النَّارِ ۞

Rabbanā ātinā fid-dunyā hasanatan wa fil ākhirati hasanatan wa qinā 'adhāban-nār.

Our Lord! Give us good in this world and good in the Hereafter and protect us from the torment of the Fire. (2:201)

رَبَّنَا لَا تُزِغْ قُلُوبَنَا بَعْدَ إِذْ هَدَيْتَنَا وَهَبْ لَنَا مِن لَّدُنْكَ رَحْمَةً ۚ إِنَّكَ أَنْتَ الْوَهَّابُ

Rabbanā lā tuzigh qulūbanā ba'da idh hadaytanā wa hab lanā milladunka rahmah, innaka Antal Wahhāb.

Our Lord! Let not our hearts stray now that You have guided us, but grant us mercy from Your Own presence, for You are the Giver (of bounties without measure). (3:8)

رَبَّنَا ظَلَمْنَا أَنْفُسَنَا وَإِنْ لَّمْ تَغْفِرْ لَنَا وَتَرْحَمْنَا لَنَكُونَنَّ مِنَ الْخَاسِرِينَ ۞

Rabbanā zalamnā anfusanā wa illam taghfir lanā wa tarhamnā lanakūnanna minal khāsirīn.

Our Lord! We have wronged ourselves and if You do not forgive us and have mercy upon us, we shall be amongst the losers. (7:23)

Sunnats Regarding Zuhr, 'Asr, Maghrib and 'Ishā Salāh

1. To perform 4 rak'āt sunnat mu'akkadah before the fardh of Zuhr and two rak'āt after fardh. *(Muslim)*

2. To perform 4 rak'āt sunnat ghair-mu'akkadah before the fardh of 'Asr Salāh. *(Tirmidhī)*

3. After the Maghrib adhān and before the fardh of Maghrib Salāh no sunnah salāh should be performed. It is however recommended to read the following du'ā:

اَللّٰهُمَّ إِنَّ هٰذَا إِقْبَالُ لَيْلِكَ وَإِدْبَارُ نَهَارِكَ وَأَصْوَاتُ دُعَاتِكَ فَاغْفِرْ لِي

Allāhumma inna hādha iqbālu laylika, wa idbāru nahārika, wa aswātu du'ātika, faghfir lī.

O Allāh! This is the hour of the advent of Your night and the retreat of Your day and the cry of Your callers, so grant me forgiveness. (Abū Dāwūd)

4. To perform 2 rak'āt sunnat mu'akkadah after the fardh of Maghrib Salāh. *(Tirmidhī)*

5. To perform 6 rak'āt of Salātul Awwābīn after the 2 rak'āt of Maghrib sunnah. One will get the reward of worshipping Allāh ﷻ for 12 years. *(Tirmidhī)*

6. To perform 4 rak'āt sunnat ghair-mu'akkadah before the fardh of 'Ishā Salāh. *(Bukhārī, Muslim)*

7. To perform 2 rak'āt sunnat mu'akkadah after the fardh of 'Ishā Salāh. (*Muslim*)

8. In the first rak'at of Witr Salāh after Sūrah Fātihah, recite Sūrah A'lā (Sūrah No 87). In the second rak'at, recite Sūrah Kāfirūn and in the third rak'at recite Sūrah Ikhlās. (*Tirmidhī, Nasa'i*)

9. To recite سُبْحَانَ الْمَلِكِ الْقُدُّوس (Subhānal Malikil Quddūs) three times softly but audibly (not so loudly as to disturb others performing salāh) after the Witr Salāh and while reading the third time to lengthen the last word i.e. Quddūs. (*Nasa'i*)

Ishrāq Salāh (Sunrise Prayer)

After Fajr Salāh, one should remain seated on the prayer mat until sunrise. 15-20 minutes after sunrise, one should perform two or four rak'āt of Ishrāq Salāh.

The reward for this is equal to one hajj and 'umrah. (*Tirmidhī*)

Breakfast

The holy Prophet ﷺ used to have honey water for breakfast. (*Umdatul Qāri - Commentary of Bukhārī*)

In some ahādīth, nabīdh-tamar has been mentioned. Nabīdh-tamar refers to dry dates which have been cut into pieces and soaked in a clay container overnight. (*Tirmidhī*)

Chāsht (Duhā) Salāh (Forenoon Prayer)

The time for Chāsht Salāh begins when the sun is bright and ends just before zawāl (midday). Chāsht Salāh ranges from two rak'āt to twelve rak'āt. *(Tirmidhī)*

In the ahādīth, many rewards have been mentioned about this salāh. One who leaves home in the state of wudhū with the intention of Chāsht salāh gets the reward of an 'umrah. *(Abū Dāwūd)*

One who performs two rak'āt of Chāsht Salāh, all his minor sins are forgiven. *(Tirmidhī)*

By performing two rak'āt of Chāsht Salāh, one will fulfil the sadaqah on behalf of the 360 joints in his body. *(Muslim)*

A huge mountain of gold will be erected for the one who performs twelve rak'āt of Chāsht Salāh. *(Ahmad)*

Sunnats of Eating

1. To wash both the hands before and after eating. *(Shamā'il)*

It was the sunnah of the prophets to wash the hands before eating. This action removes poverty. *(Majma'uz Zawāid)*

Note: The sunnah will not be fulfilled if only one hand is washed.

Washing of hands before and after meals is a means of greater goodness in one's home. *(Ibn Mājah)*

It is also a means of one's sustenance increasing. *(Kanzul 'Ummāl)*

2. To eat together. *(Abū Dāwūd)*
3. The dastarkhān (table spread) should be spread on the floor. *(Bukhārī)*

To eat on table and chairs is permissible but to sit on the floor is more closer to the sunnah.

The Prophet 	ﷺ never ate on a table, hence we should adopt the way of the Prophet ﷺ.

4. To remove footwear before eating. *(Majma'uz Zawāid)*

5. To eat in humility and sit on the floor in one of the following postures:

To squat with the buttocks away from the ground. *(Muslim)*

To sit on one leg, whilst the other knee is raised.*(Zādul Ma'ād)*

To sit on both legs as in tashahhud posture. *(Ibn Mājah)*

6. Not to lean against anything whilst eating. *(Bukhārī)*

Eating in any of the following postures is also considered as leaning and hence, discouraged:

   a. Sitting cross legged.
   b. Sitting with one hand resting on the ground.
   c. Sitting leaning to only one side.
   d. To lean against a wall.

7. To eat with the right hand. *(Bukhārī)*

Similarly, when taking food from someone, or when giving to someone, the right hand should be used. A person should not eat with the left hand as Shaytān eats and drinks with the left hand. Shaytān also joins and partakes in the food that is eaten with the left hand. *(Musnad Ahmad, Ibn Mājah)*

8.   To recite the following du'ā before eating:

بِسْمِ اللّٰهِ وَ بَرَكَةِ اللّٰهِ

Bismillāhi wa barakatillāh.

In the name of Allāh and with the blessing of Allāh. (Mustadrak Hākim)

9.   Not to take out faults of the food. *(Mu'jam al- Awsat)*

One should not criticise any halāl food. If one likes it, one should eat it, otherwise one should abstain from making any comments.

10.   To eat from the food in front of you. *(Bukhārī)*

If there are varieties of food then one can eat from other sides as well.

11.   If one forgets to read Bismillāh before eating, then he remembers whilst eating, he should recite the following du'ā:

بِسْمِ اللّٰهِ أَوَّلَهُ وَاٰخِرَهُ

Bismillāhi awwalahū wa ākhirahū.

In the name of Allāh, at the beginning and end of it. (Abū Dāwūd)

12.   Not to blow on food. *(Tirmidhī)*
13.   To clean the plate (or bowl etc.) *(Muslim, Abū Dāwūd)*

Whilst eating, if any morsel of food is left, ensure it is eaten and not left for the Shaytān. *(Muslim)*

The plate from which one eats, seeks protection from Hell for the one who cleans it thoroughly. *(Tirmidhī)*

14.   To lick the fingers three times. *(Muslim)*

15.   After eating, one should lick the fingers and then clean the plate (bowl) as it is possible that Allāh ﷻ may have kept blessings and barakah in that particle left behind on the plate or the finger. *(Muslim)*

The middle finger should be licked first, followed by the index finger and lastly, the thumb. This is when the three fingers are only used. If more than three fingers are used, then after licking the middle, index and thumb, the little and ring finger should be licked. *(Jam'ul Wasā'il)*

16.   To read the following du'ā after eating:

اَلْحَمْدُ لِلّٰهِ الَّذِيْ أَطْعَمَنَا وَسَقَانَا وَجَعَلَنَا مُسْلِمِيْنَ

Alhamdulillāhil ladhī at'amanā wa saqānā waja'alanā muslimīn.

All praises due to Allāh Who gave us food and drink and made us Muslims. (Shamā'il, Abū Dāwūd)

17. To lift the dastarkhān before one stands up. (i.e. the diners should clear up the dastarkhān, fold and lift it up before they themselves stand up.) *(Ibn Mājah)*

18. To wash the hands after eating and rinsing the mouth. *(Bukhārī)*

One should adopt moderation in eating. The Prophet ﷺ has warned against over eating. The Prophet ﷺ ate very simple and inexpensive food. *(Mustadrak Hākim)*

Sunnats of Drinking

1. To recite Bismillāh at the beginning of drinking. *(Tirmidhī)*
2. To sit down and drink water. *(Muslim)*
3. To drink with the right hand. *(Muslim)*
4. To drink water in three sips. *(Tabarānī)*
5. One should not breathe into the cup or glass, rather breathe after moving it away from the mouth. *(Bukhārī)*
6. One should not drink from the chipped end of the cup. *(Bukhārī, Abū Dāwūd)*
7. One should not drink directly from a water bottle, rather pour it into a glass or cup and drink. *(Tirmidhī)*

Note: Some narrations suggest that it is permissible to drink from a bottle, however it is more preferable not to directly drink from it. *(Tirmidhī, Dalīlul Fālihīn - Sharh Riyādhus Sālihīn)*

8. To praise Allāh ﷻ after drinking water by saying, "Alhamdulillāh".
9. To read the following du'ā after drinking water:

$$\text{اَلْحَمْدُ لِلّٰهِ الَّذِىْ سَقَانَا عَذْبًا فُرَاتًا بِرَحْمَتِهِ وَلَمْ يَجْعَلْهُ مِلْحًا أُجَاجًا بِذُنُوْبِنَا}$$

Alhamdulillāhil ladhī saqānā 'adhban furātan bi rahmatihī wa lam yaj'alhu milhan ujājan bi dhunūbinā.

All praise is due to Allāh Who gave us fresh sweet water (to drink) through His mercy and He did not make it salty or bitter due to our sins. (Kanzul 'Ummāl)

10. Amongst the drinks, Prophet ﷺ loved milk.

The Prophet ﷺ has said, "Nothing can substitute for solids and liquids at once except milk." *(Ibn Mājah)*

11. After drinking milk (or anything made with milk), this du'ā should be read:

$$ اَللّٰهُمَّ بَارِكْ لَنَا فِيْهِ وَزِدْنَا مِنْهُ $$

Allāhumma bārik lanā fīhi wa zidnā minhu.

O Allāh! Bless us in it and give us increase of it.
(Tirmidhī)

12. To gargle after drinking milk. *(Bukhārī, Ibn Mājah)*
13. Our Prophet ﷺ prohibited the usage of gold and silver utensils. *(Muslim)*
14. Our Prophet ﷺ prohibited drinking like camels in one gulp, but encouraged drinking in two or three sips. *(Tirmidhī)*
15. When distributing (anything) in a gathering, to begin with the most pious or eldest and then to distribute from the right. *(Bukhārī)*

Note: Drinking water immediately after meals is not a sunnah, especially if the water is very hot or very cold as both are harmful.

Sunnats when Leaving the Home

1. To perform two rak'āt salāh before emerging from the house. This will safeguard oneself from the outside calamities. *(Bazzār)*
2. To say salām to the members of the household when you are leaving the house. *(Bayhaqi)*
3. When leaving the home read:

بِسْمِ اللهِ تَوَكَّلْتُ عَلَى اللهِ وَلَا حَوْلَ وَلَا قُوَّةَ إِلَّا بِاللهِ

Bismillāhi tawakkaltu 'alallāhi, wa lā hawla wa lā quwwata illā billāh.

In the name of Allāh, I depend on Allāh, and there is no power (to do good) nor restraint (to avoid evil) except with Allāh.

When anyone reads this du'ā, the angels say to him, "You have been guided and have been saved (from all harm)." *(Abū Dāwūd, Tirmidhī)*

Sayyidah Umme Salamah ؓ says, "Whenever the Prophet ﷺ left my house, he used to raise his eyes towards the heavens and read the following du'ā:

اَللّٰهُمَّ إِنِّيْ أَعُوْذُ بِكَ أَنْ أَضِلَّ أَوْ أُضَلَّ أَوْ أَزِلَّ أَوْ أُزَلَّ أَوْ أَظْلِمَ أَوْ أُظْلَمَ أَوْ أَجْهَلَ أَوْ يُجْهَلَ عَلَيَّ

Allāhumma innī a'ūdhubika an adilla aw udalla, aw azilla aw uzalla, aw adlima aw udlama, aw ajhala aw yujhala 'alayya.

O Allāh! I seek Your protection from misleading and being misled, from causing someone to slip or slipping, from oppressing and oppression and from promoting ignorance and being foolish. (Abū Dāwūd, Tirmidhī)

Sunnats when Entering the Home

1. To read any dhikr of Allāh ﷻ whilst entering the house. *(Muslim)*

Note: If Allāh ﷻ is not remembered when entering the house, then the Shaytān announces to his subordinates, "Come, we have found accommodation for the night." *(Muslim)*

2. The following du'ā should be read at the time of entering the house:

اَللّٰهُمَّ إِنِّيْ أَسْأَلُكَ خَيْرَ الْمَوْلَجِ وَخَيْرَ الْمَخْرَجِ بِسْمِ اللهِ وَلَجْنَا وَبِسْمِ اللهِ خَرَجْنَا وَعَلَى اللهِ رَبِّنَا تَوَكَّلْنَا

Allāhumma innī as'aluka khayral mawlaji, wa khayral makhraji, Bismillāhi wa lajnā, wa Bismillāhi kharajnā, wa 'alallāhi Rabbinā tawakkalnā.

O Allāh! I ask You the blessing of entering and leaving. In Allāh's name we enter and in Allāh's name we leave and in Allāh, our Lord, we trust.
(Abū Dāwūd)

3. Salām should be said to the members of the household. (24:61)
4. To announce one has arrived at home by knocking on the door or coughing etc. *(Nasa'i)*

Note: The reason for such announcement is to inform the member of the family sitting in a way that could cause embarrassment to them if one were to suddenly enter.

5. To enter the house with the right foot. *(Bukhārī)*
6. To perform miswāk after entering the house. *(Muslim, Abū Dāwūd)*
7. After entering the house, perform two rak'āt salāh which will safeguard one from any calamities of the house. *(Bazzār)*

Sunnats for Night Time

1. To sleep in the state of wudhū. If one is already in the state of wudhū, then it would not be necessary to refresh the wudhū. *(Bukhārī)*
2. To recite Bismillāh whilst closing the doors or locking them. *(Bukhārī)*
3. To sleep early at night. The holy Prophet ﷺ used to dislike sleeping before 'Ishā and talking after Ishā Salāh. *(Bukhārī)*

Therefore, if there is no important work, one should go to sleep early so he can wake up for Tahajjud and Fajr Salāh.

4. To cover or put away all utensils. *(Muslim)*
5. To extinguish or switch off any lights or burning fire which may catch alight (if left on). *(Musnad Bazzār)*
6. To remove any kind of sticky substance, wax etc. left on the hands or feet. *(Abū Dāwūd)*
7. To dust the bedding before sleeping. *(Bukhārī)*
8. To apply surma (antimony). The holy Prophet ﷺ used to apply ithmid surma three times on his right eye and then thrice on his left eye. *(Shamā'il Tirmidhī)*
9. To do tawbah (repentance) before going to sleep. *(Tirmidhī)*
10. To sleep in the state that one removes jealousy and enmity from one's heart. *(Tirmidhī)*

11. To sleep with the intention of waking up for Tahajjud. If a person doesn't wake up for Tahajjud, even then he will get the reward for his good intention. *(Nasa'i)*

12. To read the different du'ās at the time of sleeping.

اَللّٰهُمَّ بِاسْمِكَ أَمُوْتُ وَأَحْيَا

Allāhumma bismika amūtu wa ahyā.

O Allāh! By Your name I live and I die. (Bukhārī, Muslim)

اَللّٰهُمَّ أَسْلَمْتُ نَفْسِيْ إِلَيْكَ وَوَجَّهْتُ وَجْهِيْ إِلَيْكَ وَفَوَّضْتُ أَمْرِيْ إِلَيْكَ وَأَلْجَأْتُ ظَهْرِيْ إِلَيْكَ رَغْبَةً وَّرَهْبَةً إِلَيْكَ لَا مَلْجَأَ وَلَا مَنْجَا مِنْكَ إِلَّا إِلَيْكَ أَمَنْتُ بِكِتَابِكَ الَّذِيْ أَنْزَلْتَ وَبِنَبِيِّكَ الَّذِيْ أَرْسَلْتَ

Allāhumma aslamtu nafsī ilayka, wa wajjahtu wajhī ilayka, wa fawwadtu amrī ilayka, wa al-ja'tu zahrī ilayka, raghbatan wa rahbatan ilayka, lā malja'a wa lā manjā minka illā ilayka, āmantu bi kitābikal-ladhī anzalta wa bi nabiyyi kalladhī arsalta.

O Allāh! I have surrendered my life to You, and turned my face towards You, and entrusted all my affairs to You, and wholly placed my reliance in You. (All this I do) to gain Your mercy and due to fear of Your punishment. There is no protection from Your wrath except through Your mercy. I believe in the book You have revealed and in the Prophet You have sent."

46

Whoever recites this du'ā, then passes away in the night will be counted as having passed away on Islām. If he wakes up in the morning, he will wake up on goodness. *(Bukhārī, Muslim)*

اَللّٰهُمَّ قِنِيْ عَذَابَكَ يَوْمَ تَبْعَثُ عِبَادَكَ

Allāhumma qinī 'adhābaka yawma tab'athu 'ibādaka.

O Allāh! Save me from Your punishment on the day You will raise Your servants. (Abū Dāwūd)

13. To recite Āyatul Kursī. The benefit of reciting this is that an angel will be appointed to protect the reader. Shaytān will not come close to him. *(Bukhārī)*
14. To recite the last two verses of Sūrah Baqarah; this will suffice him from all other things. *(Bukhārī)*
15. To recite Sūrah Kāfirūn. *(Abū Dāwūd)*
16. To recite Sūrah Ikhlās, Sūrah Falaq and Sūrah Nās. The Prophet ﷺ used to recite these three sūrahs and blow on his palms. Thereafter, he would wipe both his hands on his face and entire body where his hands could reach. *(Bukhārī)*
17. To recite Sūrah Sajdah and Sūrah Mulk. *(Tirmidhī)*
18. To recite Sūrah Wāqi'ah before sleeping, this will safeguard a person from hunger and poverty. *(Bayhaqi Shua'bul Imān)*
19. To recite the Tasbīh Fātimi. *(Abū Dāwūd)*
    - Thirty-three times, "Subhān'Allāh"
    - Thirty-three times, "Alhamdulillāh"

- Thirty-four times, "Allāhu Akbar" *(Tirmidhī)*

20. To sleep on the right-hand side (facing towards the qiblah) and to sleep with the right hand under the cheek. *(Abū Dāwūd)*

21. To continue doing dhikr until sleep overtakes one.

ٱلَّذِيۡنَ يَذۡكُرُوۡنَ اللّٰهَ قِيَامًا وَّقُعُوۡدًا وَّعَلٰى جُنُوۡبِهِمۡ ۞

(The intelligent are those) who remember their Lord standing, sitting and lying down (in all postures). (3:191)

22. To do miswāk even though one has already done it for 'Ishā Salāh. *(Kanzul 'Ummāl)*

Also to do miswāk when the eyes open. *(Bukhārī, Muslim)*

23. The Prophet ﷺ has prohibited sleeping on the stomach. This is the Shaytān's method of sleeping and Allāh ﷻ dislikes this position of sleeping. *(Abū Dāwūd)*

24. The Prophet ﷺ prohibited sleeping lying flat on the back with one leg on the other. *(Tirmidhī)*

Note: If there is no fear of exposing the private parts then it is permissible to lie down in this manner.

25. The Prophet ﷺ prohibited sleeping on such a roof top that does not have a safety wall. *(Abū Dāwūd)*

26. One should not sleep in any such places that cause inconvenience to others. For example;

    - On any road or pathways
    - In front of doorways
    - In the midst of gatherings. *(Majma'uz Zawāid)*

Sunnats of Salām (Greeting)

1. To spread salām amongst the people. *(Bukhārī)*
2. To use the Islamic greeting (Assalāmu 'alaykum wa rahmatullāhi wa barakātuh) to greet someone. Do not use any other method of greeting. *(Bukhārī)*
3. To greet with the full salām which will earn the person 30 rewards and to reply with the same (wa 'alaykumus salām wa rahmatullāhi wa barakātuh). *(Tirmidhī)*
4. Always try to precede others in salām. The one who initiates salām obtains greater reward. *(Muslim)*
5. Salām should be done before engaging in conversation. *(Tirmidhī*
6. To repeat the salām three times if there is no response. *(Bukhārī)*

Note: When visiting any home, it is sunnah to seek permission to enter by saying salām thrice. The Prophet 🕌 commanded to seek permission thrice and if one receives no response after the third salām, then to return. *(Bukhārī)*

7. Youngsters should greet the elders, the one who is riding should greet those walking and those who are walking should greet the sitting, and the small group should greet the big group. *(Bukhārī)*
8. To greet children. *(Bukhārī)*
9. The meeting and greeting should be with a smile. *(Muslim, Tirmidhī)*
10. One should greet every person i.e. those whom he knows and

those whom he doesn't know. *(Bukhārī)*

11. To greet the person again from whom one had parted company, even if such parting was for a short while. *(Abū Dāwūd)*

12. To greet when entering or leaving the home (whether it is one's own home or that of another). *(Abū Dāwūd)*

13. At night, the Prophet ﷺ greeted so softly that those who were asleep were not disturbed and those who were awake could hear. *(Tirmidhī)*

14. The Prophet ﷺ sent back a Companion who entered without having greeted or having sought permission (hence it is sunnah to educate one's junior in such a manner). *(Tirmidhī)*

15. If a third person's salām are conveyed to one, then it should be answered in the following manner:

وَعَلَيْكَ وَعَلَيْهِ السَّلَامُ

Wa 'alayka wa 'alayhis salām

Peace be upon you and him. *(Abū Dāwūd)*

Some of the Ādāb of Salām

1. Adopt the practice of mutual salām. Upon meeting a Muslim, say, "Assalāmu'alaykum". In reply, say, "Wa 'alaykumus salām".

2. One person from a group making salām will act as a representative for the whole group. His salām will be adequate on behalf of the group.

3. When replying to the salām of a person, the salām should be made verbally, not by a sign of the hand or a nod of the head.
4. It is wājib to reply to the salām (in normal situations).
5. A person who is engaged in a conversation or in some other work should not be greeted.
6. It is not permissible to bow and make salām.
7. When answering the call of nature, neither reply to anyone's salām, nor offer anyone salām.
8. On promising to convey someone's salām, it becomes wājib to do so.
9. When making salām to elders, adopt a low voice. Do not express yourself in such terms that show arrogance or disrespect.

Sunnats of Musāfahah (Handshake)

1. Whilst shaking hands, the following du'ā should be read:

يَغْفِرُ اللهُ لَنَا وَلَكُمْ

Yaghfirullāhu lanā wa lakum

May Allāh forgive us and you. (Abū Dāwūd)

2. Both hands should be used in musāfahah. It is insufficient to let one's fingers touch those of the other. Palms should be firmly grasped. *(Bukhārī)*
3. Women should also greet each other by shaking hands. *(Bayhaqi)*
4. The Prophet ﷺ would not withdraw his hands from the person who was shaking it until the other removed his hands. Furthermore, the Prophet ﷺ would not turn his face away from anybody. *(Tirmidhī)*
5. Sayyidunā Anas ؓ used to rub scented oil on his hands every day for the sake of doing musāfahah with people. *(Al-Adabul Mufrad)*
5. To shake hands when departing also. *(Tirmidhī)*
6. The Prophet ﷺ has said that by shaking hands, Allāh ﷻ removes malice (between people). *(Targhīb)*

Virtues of Musāfahah

1. Allāh ﷻ forgives the sins of those who shake hands even before their hands part. *(Tirmidhī)*
2. When two Muslims meet and shake hands, their sins shed away as leaves shed off a tree. *(Targhīb)*
3. Sayyidunā Abū Dharr ؓ narrates that he could not remember an occasion when the Prophet ﷺ greeted him and did not shake his hands. *(Abū Dāwūd)*

Sunnats Regarding Mu'ānaqah (Hugging) and Embracing

1. Sayyidah 'Ā'ishah ﷺ narrates that Sayyidunā Zaid ibn Hārithah ﷺ arrived in Madīnah Munawwarah and the Prophet ﷺ was at home. He knocked on the door, and (upon hearing who it was), the Prophet ﷺ rushed towards the door. He met Zaid ﷺ, hugged him and kissed him. (*Tirmidhī*)

   Note: Sayyidunā Zaid ibn Hārithah ﷺ was the Prophet's ﷺ adopted son.

2. Sayyidunā Ja'far ﷺ narrates that when he arrived in Madīnah Munawwarah, the Prophet ﷺ hugged and kissed him between his forehead. (*Abū Dāwūd*)

3. The Companions ﷺ used to shake hands when meeting one another and when anyone returned from a journey, they would hug one another. (*Tahāwī*)

4. The Prophet ﷺ used to hug his grandsons and kiss them. (*Bukhārī, Muslim*)

5. When Sayyidah Fātimah ﷺ, the beloved daughter of the holy Prophet ﷺ would visit him, he would stand up to receive her. The Prophet ﷺ would take her by her hand, kiss her and seat her where he was sat. Sayyidah Fātimah ﷺ would do the same when the Prophet ﷺ visited her. (*Abū Dāwūd*)

6. Sayyidunā Salamah ibn Akwa ﷺ narrates that he kissed the Prophet's ﷺ blessed hand on the occasion when he pledged

allegiance to him. *(Majma')*

7. It is sunnah to kiss the hands of the pious and senior scholars. *(Abū Dāwūd)*

Sunnats Regarding Clothing

Allāh ﷻ says:

يٰبَنِيٓ اٰدَمَ قَدۡ اَنۡزَلۡنَا عَلَيۡكُمۡ لِبَاسًا يُّوَارِيۡ سَوۡاٰتِكُمۡ وَرِيۡشًا ۖ وَلِبَاسُ التَّقۡوٰى ۙ ذٰلِكَ خَيۡرٌ ۚ
ذٰلِكَ مِنۡ اٰيٰتِ اللّٰهِ لَعَلَّهُمۡ يَذَّكَّرُوۡنَ ۞

"O children of Ādam! We have indeed sent clothing down to you, so that you may conceal the private parts of your bodies and as a means of beautification." (7:26)

Sayyidah Umme Salamah ﷺ narrates that the clothing the Prophet ﷺ loved the most was the qamīs (long shirt). *(Abū Dāwūd, Tirmidhī)*

Mulla Alī Qāri ﷺ has written that qamīs (long shirt) is more concealing, lighter on the body and it displays humility.

1. The Prophet ﷺ wore a qamīs that was above his ankles reaching up to his midcalf. *(Ibn Mājah)*
2. The sleeves of the qamīs (kurta) used to reach up to his fingers. *(Tirmidhī)*. In some narrations up to the wrists. *(Abū Dāwūd)*

Sayyidunā Abū Hurairah ؓ narrates that the Prophet ﷺ said that the part of the trousers that goes beyond the ankles will surely be in the Fire of Hell. *(Bukhārī)*

Note: This ruling is for the males only. Females must cover their ankles with their dress. A Muslim male should always refrain from lowering one's garment beyond the ankles, whether in salāh or out of salāh, be it pyjamas, lunghi or jubbas.

3. Wear white clothes. *(Abū Dāwūd, Tirmidhī)*
A person can wear clothes of different colours, but according to the sunnah (for males) white colour is preferable.

In one hadīth, the holy Prophet ﷺ says, "Wear white clothes. Verily it is cleaner and purer, and you should shroud your dead in it." *(Nasa'i)*

4. To wear clean and new clothes on Friday. *(Abū Dāwūd)*
5. Not to wear clothes for showing off. *(Abū Dāwūd)*
6. The holy Prophet ﷺ prohibited wearing clothes that had pictures of animate objects. *(Bukhārī)*
7. The Prophet ﷺ prohibited adopting the styles exclusively to the non-Muslims in clothing. *(Muslim)*
8. Men should not imitate the clothing of women and the women should not imitate the clothing of men. *(Abū Dāwūd)*
9. It is prohibited for the male to wear clothing of silk and gold but it is permissible for the female. *(Ahmad)*

10. The holy Prophet ﷺ wore clothes that had buttons and a collar. *(Abū Dāwūd, Ibn Mājah)*

11. To commence wearing the clothing from the right side. Therefore, when wearing the qamīs, the Prophet ﷺ would wear the right sleeve before the left. This is the sunnah procedure for wearing garments and shoes - the right limb should be worn first. Similarly, when removing any garment, the left side should be removed before the right. *(Abū Dāwūd, Nasa'i, Mustadrak)*

12. The Prophet ﷺ used to wear a white hat and white turban at home, and a black turban on a journey. *(Tabarānī)*

13. The holy Prophet ﷺ said, "The distinction between us and the non-believers is the wearing of turbans upon the hat." *(Tirmidhī, Abū Dāwūd)*

14. Trousers and lunghi should be tied slightly below the navel in such a manner that it would seem as if it was on the navel. *(Musnad Ahmad, Ibn Hibbān)*

15. The Prophet ﷺ said, "Wear trousers, as it is more effective in concealing the satr." *(Kanzul 'Ummāl)*

16. The Prophet ﷺ encouraged women to wear trousers (loose salwar) (under their jilbāb) when they leave their homes.

17. The sunnah clothing of a woman is:
    - It should be thick
    - It should not be transparent
    - It should be loose and not tight fitting
    - It should not resemble male clothing
    - It should not resemble the exclusive clothing of non–Muslims. *(Bukhārī, Muslim, Abū Dāwūd, Muwatta Mālik)*

18. When putting on clothing, the following du'ā should be read:

اَلْحَمْدُ لِلّٰهِ الَّذِيْ كَسَانِيْ هٰذَا وَرَزَقَنِيْهِ مِنْ غَيْرِ حَوْلٍ مِّنِّيْ وَلَا قُوَّةٍ

Alhamdulillāh hil-ladhī kasānī hādhā wa razaqanīhi min ghayri hawlim minnī wa lā quwwatin.

"Praise be to Allāh Who clothed me in this and gave it to me without any effort and strength on my part."

Whoever recites this du'ā, his past and present sins will be forgiven. (*Abū Dāwūd, Tirmidhī*)

19. When putting on new clothing, the following du'ā should be read:

اَلْحَمْدُ لِلّٰهِ الَّذِيْ كَسَانِيْ مَا أُوَارِيْ بِهِ عَوْرَتِيْ وَأَتَجَمَّلُ بِهِ فِيْ حَيَاتِيْ

Alhamdulillāhil-ladhī kasānī mā uwārī bihī 'awratī wa ata jammalu bihī fi hayātī.

"Praise be to Allāh Who clothed me with what covers my nakedness and with that, by which I adorn myself in my life." (*Tirmidhī, Ibn Mājah*)

20. Before removing clothing at the time of sleep or changing etc, the following du'ā should be read:

بِسْمِ اللّٰهِ الَّذِيْ لَا اِلٰهَ اِلَّا هُوَ

Bismillāhil ladhī lā ilāha illā Hū.

"In the name of Allāh, besides Whom there is no god." (*Ibnus Sunni*)

21. When observing someone wear new clothes, recite:

اِلْبَسْ جَدِيْدًا وَعِشْ حَمِيْدًا وَمُتْ شَهِيْدًا

Ilbas jadīdan, wa 'ish hamīdan, wa mut shahīdan.
"May you wear new clothing, live well and die a martyr!" (Ibn Mājah)

22. The Prophet ﷺ wore strapped leather sandals. *(Abū Dāwūd)*

23. The Prophet ﷺ wore leather socks, both at home and when on a journey. *(Muslim)*

24. The Prophet ﷺ prohibited walking with one shoe only. *(Bukhārī)*

25. When wearing shoes or clothing, one should begin with the right, and when removing them to begin with the left. *(Tirmidhī)*

26. Whenever the Prophet ﷺ lifted his shoes, he did so with his index finger and thumb of his left hand. *(Tabarānī)*

Sunnats Regarding the Hair

1.   Sayyidunā Anas ﷺ reports that the Prophet's ﷺ hair was between the ears and the shoulder. *(Bukhārī)*

According to the ahādīth, three terms have been used describing the length of the Prophet's ﷺ hair:
   A.   Wafrah, which refers to the hair that extends till the earlobe. *(Abū Dāwūd)*
   B.   Limmah, which refers to the hair that goes beyond the earlobe. *(Bukhārī, Muslim)*
   C.   Jummah, which refers to the hair that extends till the shoulders. *(Bazzār, Tabarāni)*

The Prophet's ﷺ hair generally used to be between the earlobe and the shoulder. The differences in the ahādīth refer to the gradual growth or cutting of the hair. In other words, wafrah refers to the time when the hair was cut and jummah refers to the time when it had grown to its full length. *(Nasa'i, Abū Dāwūd, Tirmidhī, Ibn Mājah)*

When keeping long hair, it is preferable to have a parting in the middle of the hair. Our beloved Prophet ﷺ would not let his hair extend beyond the shoulders. *(Bukhārī)*

2.   When shaving the head, one should begin from the right. The entire right side should be shaved first and thereafter, one should commence shaving the left side. This is due to

61

beginning all good things with the right side. *(Bukhārī)*

3.   The Prophet ﷺ said:

مَنْ كَانَ لَه شَعْرٌ فَلْيُكْرِمْهُ

"He who has hair should groom it." *(Abū Dāwūd)*

Hence, it is recommended for one to keep his hair clean and groomed, especially if it is long.

4.   The Prophet ﷺ disliked untidiness in the keeping of the hair and beard. *(Abū Dāwūd)*
5.   The Prophet ﷺ used to oil his hair very often. To prevent his hat and turban from staining, he had a special cloth that was used to prevent other garments from being stained. *(Shamā'il)*
6.   When the Prophet ﷺ intended to put oil on his hair, he used to place the oil in his left palm and with his fingers, he would firstly apply a little portion of oil on his eyebrows and then on the eyelids and lastly, on the head. *(Kanzul 'Ummāl)*
7.   For children, it is preferable not to keep long hair. *(Abū Dāwūd)*
8.   The Prophet ﷺ has prohibited the adding of hair extensions to one's own hair. *(Muslim)*
9.   The Prophet ﷺ used a mirror when combing his beard or hair. *(Mu'jamul Awsat)*
10. The moustache should be trimmed so that the hair does not flow over the lip. *(Bayhaqi)*
11. It is preferable to trim the moustache to such an extent that the

skin beneath the hair becomes visible. *(Bukhārī)*

12. When applying oil to the beard, our Prophet 🕮 used to begin with the baby beard i.e. the hair between the lower lip and chin. *(Nasa'i)*

13. To trim the beard beyond one fist length if it becomes long. *(Tirmidhī)*

Note 1: It is permissible to dye the white hair with henna (mendhi) or saffron. It is prohibited to use black dye on the hair whether of the beard or head.

Note 2: Women must not cut their hair up and above their shoulders. Treating split ends by slightly trimming them is permissible.

Note 3: The hair must be of an equal length all over the head.

14. Sayyidunā 'Abdullāh ibn 'Umar 🕮 narrates that the Prophet 🕮 prohibited them from qaza. The narrator enquired about the meaning of the word and he was informed that qaza means to shave a portion of the hair and retain the rest. *(Muslim)*

Imām Nawawi 🕮 has written that any hairstyle where the hair is partially shaved or shortened and the rest is maintained is categorised as qaza. This is fashionable among the youth and it is clearly prohibited.

Note: On wearing a wig: Sayyidah 'Ā'ishah ⬥ narrates that a woman came to the Prophet ⬥ and informed him that her daughter who was going to be married on that day, had patches on her head due to falling hair. She asked the Prophet ⬥ if she could use the trimmed hair of another woman and join it to her daughter so that it would not seem awful. The Prophet ⬥ said, "Allāh has cursed the woman who joins hair to other people's hair, and the one to whose others hair is joined." *(Nasa'i)*

Note: Wigs or hair extensions made from human or pig's hair is not permitted. However animal hair (other than pig) or synthetic fibre is permissible.

Sunnats Regarding the Beard

Sayyidunā Jābir ibn Samurah ◈ reports that the Prophet's ◈ beard was dense and thick. *(Muslim)*

1. It is sunnah to comb the beard. Sayyidunā Anas ◈ narrates that the Prophet ◈ used to apply oil excessively to his blessed head and he used to comb his beard. *(Tirmidhī, Shamā'il)*
2. Sayyidah 'Ā'ishah ◈ narrates that the Prophet ◈ used to look into the mirror when combing his blessed beard. *(Majma', Fathul Bārī)*
3. Sayyidah 'Ā'ishah ◈ narrates that the Prophet ◈ always carried the following five items whether he was at home or abroad: a mirror, a kuhl (antimony) container, a comb, hair oil and miswāk. *(Tabarānī, Bayhaqi)*

Note: These items are always required. If a person carries them with him in emulation of the sunnah, he will receive great reward.

4. The Prophet ◈ would arrange his beard by applying water to it. *(Shu'abul Īmān)*
5. The Prophet ◈ would apply musk perfume to his blessed beard and head. *(Bukhārī, Muslim)*
6. To rub the itr (perfume) on ones palm before applying on ones beard. *(Bukhārī)*
7. The Prophet ◈ would dye his blessed beard with saffron. *(Nasa'i)*

8.   When the Prophet ﷺ was overcome with anxiety or grief, he would clutch his beard. *(Majma', Bazzār)*

9.   To shave the baby beard is an innovation. The baby beard refers to the hair between the lower lip and chin. Sayyidunā Anas ﷺ narrates that a few strands of the Prophet's ﷺ baby beard was white. *(Muslim)*

10.   It is sunnah to trim the beard if it is too long. The Prophet ﷺ used to shorten the length and width of his blessed beard. *(Tirmidhī)*

Note: The minimum valid length of the beard is the equivalent of a fist. A beard that is shorter than this is invalid.

It is makrūh to pluck white hair from one's beard or head. The Prophet ﷺ said, "Do not remove white hair, as it is a source of light for a believer. If a Muslim's hair turns white, one good deed is recorded for him, one sin is forgiven and Allāh ﷻ will raise his status." *(Abū Dāwūd,)*

Ruling: All the prophets kept beards and none of them shaved it, nor did they keep fine stubble on their faces. All the imāms and scholars of Islām unanimously regard the growing of a beard as wājib. The beard is an adornment for a man. *(Hidāya)*

No jurists have permitted a beard that is less than a fist length. It is harām to cut the beard when it is less than a fist length.

Note: Having a goatee beard or pencil line beard is not permissible.

Sunnats Regarding the Moustache

Sayyidunā Abū Hurairah ﷺ narrates that the Prophet ﷺ said, "Five things are from fitrah (nature); circumcision, shaving the pubic hair, trimming the moustache, clipping the nails and removing the hair of the armpits." *(Bukhārī)*

1. To trim the moustache. The Prophet ﷺ would trim the moustache very finely. *(Majma')*
2. The hair of the moustache should not be allowed to reach the upper lip. *(Tabarānī, Bayhaqi)*
3. It is preferable to trim the moustache to such an extent that the skin beneath the hair becomes visible. *(Bukhārī)*
4. To trim the moustache before the Jumu'ah Salāh. *(Tabarānī)*

Islām has instructed us to be the cleanest on Fridays; hence it is better to cut the moustache and nails on a Friday. However, if the need arises before a Friday, then one should not delay in carrying out these tasks.

Warning: The Prophet ﷺ said, "Whoever does not remove pubic hair, trim the moustache and cut the nails is not of us." *(Kanzul Ummāl)* The Prophet ﷺ is informing us that he is not a complete believer. Hence, by carrying out these acts, we are following the true spirit of Islām, as well as keeping ourselves clean and tidy.

Sunnats Regarding the Nails

1. To cut the fingernails and toenails on Friday. *(Kanzul 'Ummāl)*
2. It is makrūh (disliked) to dispose the nails in a filthy place. *(Mirqāt)*
3. It is mustahab (preferable) to bury the nails. *(Kanzul 'Ummāl, Fathul Bārī)*

Note: (1) One should be careful not to leave nails lying about as people could utilise them for witchcraft purposes. (2) Do not bite the nails. It is unhygienic and could cause sickness and poverty. *(Shāmi)*

Time Duration for Cutting Nails

Nails should be cut on a weekly basis (as well as the trimming of the moustache and pubic hair). The Prophet ﷺ used to cut the nails on a weekly basis. If one cannot clean the pubic hair weekly, it should be done once in two weeks and it should not be delayed beyond forty days, as warnings have been mentioned against this. Fifteen days is the average and forty days is the maximum limit. *(Mirqāt)*

Sunnats Regarding Itr (Perfume)

The Prophet ﷺ has stated, "Four actions are from the noble habits of the prophets; (1) To use miswāk (2) circumcision (3) to apply itr (perfume) and (4) nikāh (marriage)." (*Tirmidhī*)

1.   The Prophet ﷺ would not refuse itr as a gift. (*Bukhārī*)

Sayyidunā 'Abdullāh ibn 'Umar ؓ narrates that the Prophet ﷺ said, "Three things should not be refused; pillow, milk and itr." (*Tirmidhī*)

2.   Sayyidunā Anas ibn Mālik ؓ narrates, "Never did I smell musk or amber or any other fragrance that was sweeter than the Prophet's ﷺ natural fragrance." (*Muslim*)

3.   Sayyidah 'Ā'ishah ؓ used to apply perfume to our Prophet ﷺ. (*Bukhārī*)

Hence, it is sunnah for a wife to apply perfume on her husband. She could also apply perfume on her husband's clothes.

4.   We should apply itr at the following occasions;
   - On the day of Jumu'ah (*Bukhārī, Muslim*)
   - On both days of 'Īd (*Jam'ul Wasā'il, Hidāyah*)
   - At the time of Tahajjud (*Bazzār*)
   - After wudhū (*Majma'uz Zawāid*)
   - When wearing ihrām (*Bukhārī, Muslim*)
   - At the time of reciting the Qur'ān (*Jam'ul Wasā'il*)

- At the time of teaching and learning *(Jam'ul Wasā'il)*
- At the time of dhikr *(Jam'ul Wasā'il)*
- When going to any gatherings *(Jam'ul Wasā'il, Hidāyah)*
- Before narrating ahādīth *(Majma'uz Zawāid)*
- When the husband and wife meet *(Bukhārī, Muslim)*
- When a woman takes a bath after menstruation or post-natal bleeding *(Bukhārī, Muslim)*

5. The Prophet 鸞 loved 'ūd, amber and musk the most from all the types of itr. *(Muslim, Tirmidhī)*

6. The itr for males is that which has a dominant fragrance and very little colour whilst for females it is that which has very little smell and more colour. *(Tirmidhī)*

7. It is sunnah to offer people perfume as a gift *(Majma'uz Zawāid)*

Sayyidah Zainab 鸞 narrates that the Prophet 鸞 said, "The best way of honouring a Muslim is by offering him perfume, it is not burdensome (to accept) and it has a pleasant smell." *(Majma'uz Zawāid)*

8. It is sunnah to have a perfume container. *(Bayhaqi)*

Sunnats Regarding Surmah (Antimony)

Sayyidunā 'Abdullāh ibn 'Abbās ﷺ narrates that the holy Prophet ﷺ would apply ithmid (surmah) thrice to his eyes before sleeping. *(Shamā'il)*

1. It is sunnah to use surmah (collyrium) before sleeping. *(Shamā'il)*
2. It is sunnah to apply surmah thrice to each eye. *(Shamā'il)*
3. It is best to apply ithmid kuhl (surmah). *(Shamā'il)*

Note: Ithmid is a type of surmah that has special benefits. The 'ulamā' (scholars) are of the opinion that it is a reference to the kuhl of Isfahān. They have also mentioned that its usage is highly recommended in respect of people who have good eyesight. People with poor eyesight should not use it, as it would cause aggravation. *(Khasā'il Nabawi)*

4. Three sunnah methods of applying kuhl have been reported regarding the Prophet ﷺ:
    a. Three strokes in each eye.
    b. Three in the right eye and two strokes in the left eye.
    c. Two in each eye, and a third to both without re-inserting (dipping) the stick for more surmah.

Similarly, a person has the choice of applying and completing one eye first, or he could alternate the application to both the eyes. *(Jam'ul Wasā'il)*

5.   It is sunnah to carry and apply kuhl whilst on a journey.

Sayyidah 'Ā'ishah ﷺ narrates that the Prophet ﷺ always kept the following five items with him whether he was at home or abroad; a mirror, a kuhl container, a comb, hair oil and a miswāk. *(Tabarānī, Bayhaqi)*

Note: It is sunnah to carry these items whilst on a journey. Certain narrations mention a pair of scissors as well as a little stick, which would be used for scratching hard-to-reach areas of the body.

Sunnats Regarding Travelling

Sayyidunā Abū Hurairah ؓ narrates that the holy Prophet ﷺ said, "Travel and you will remain healthy." *(Kanzul 'Ummāl)*

1.   Travelling is a means of acquiring good health. *(al-Jāmi'us-Saghīr)*
2.   Travel is a fraction of difficulty. It prevents one from one's normal routine of sleeping, eating and drinking. Thus, when anyone has accomplished the purpose of his travel, he should hasten back to his house. *(Bukhārī)*
3.   To commence one's journey on a Thursday. *(Bukhārī)*

Note: Although the Prophet ﷺ commenced his journeys on other days, he loved commencing journeys on Thursdays.

4.   One should seek a companion before undertaking a journey.

Sayyidunā 'Alī ؓ narrates that the Prophet ﷺ said:

a.   "Search for a neighbour before building a house
b.   A travel companion before the journey
c.   Make adequate arrangements for your journey before departing." (Ithāf) *(Daylami)*

5.   One should carry food provisions for the journey. *(Bukhārī)*
6.   To perform two rak'āt of salāh before setting out on a journey. *(Majma'uz Zawāid)*

7. Our Prophet 🕌 discouraged setting out alone on a journey. *(Bukhārī)*

8. Our Prophet 🕌 has advised us to appoint an amīr (leader) when several people are travelling together so that decisions could be easily reached after mashwura (consultation). *(Abū Dāwūd)*

9. To request the one going on a journey for du'ās. *(Abū Dāwūd, Tirmidhī)*

Sayyidunā 'Abdullāh ibn 'Umar 🕌 narrates that when Sayyidunā 'Umar 🕌 sought permission from the Prophet 🕌 to travel for the sake of performing 'umrah, the Prophet 🕌 permitted him to go and said, "Do not forget us in your righteous supplications." *(Abū Dāwūd)*

10. To take one's wife along on a journey. *(Bukhārī)*

11. To keep the following items on a journey; mirror, surmah container, comb, miswāk and a small stick for scratching the back. *(Bayhaqi, Kanzul 'Ummāl)*

12. If possible, to take an assistant or helper on a journey. *(Bukhārī)*

13. Death whilst on a journey merits the reward of a martyr. *(Ibn Mājah)*

14. Whilst on a journey, our Prophet 🕌 used to recite shorter surahs in salāh. *(Abū Dāwūd. Musannaf)*

15. To perform nafl (optional) salāh whilst sitting on one's transport, facing the direction in which one is moving. *(Bukhārī)*

Note: Whilst travelling, a person may perform nafl salāh in or on his conveyance or other mode of transport. Indications of the head suffice for the posture of rukūʿ and sajdah. The salāh can be performed in the direction being travelled instead of facing the qiblah. This exception to the general procedure of salāh is only applied to optional and non-obligatory salāh.

16. To fast and not to fast on a journey is also a sunnah. *(Bukhārī)*
17. To help and assist one's companions whilst on a journey cannot be surpassed by any actions save shahādat (martyrdom). *(Bukhārī, Muslim)*
18. To meet and greet one's relatives and friends before departing on a journey. *(Majmaʿuz Zawāid)*
19. To accompany the departing traveller for a short distance and to advise and make duʿā for him. *(Hākim)*
20. As a recommendation, one must constantly engage in dhikr (remembrance of Allāh ﷻ) during a journey.

Sayyidunā ʿUqbah ibn Āmir ؓ narrates that the Prophet ﷺ said, "If a person engages in the dhikr of Allāh ﷻ during his journey, the angels travel with him during that journey, and if he engages in singing (or listening to un-Islamic) poems and lyrics, the devil remains his companion." *(Kanzul ʿUmmāl)*

Note: In today's time, people would rather listen to music and songs whilst travelling instead of engaging in dhikr actively or passively. Thus, devils will be travelling with them instead of angels.

21. Before setting out on a journey one should meet one's friends and relatives who should make du'ā for him in the following words:

اَسْتَوْدِعُ اللهَ دِيْنَكَ وَاَمَانَتَكَ وَخَوَاتِيْمَ عَمَلِكَ

Astawdi 'ullāha dīnaka wa amānataka wa khawātīma 'amalika.

I entrust Allāh with your religion, your belongings and the result of your deeds. (Abū Dāwūd)

22. When leaving home, on the commencement of a journey one should read the following du'ā:

بِسْمِ اللهِ تَوَكَّلْتُ عَلَى اللهِ اَللّٰهُمَّ إِنَّا نَعُوْذُ بِكَ مِنْ أَنْ نَّزِلَّ أَوْ نَضِلَّ أَوْ نَظْلِمَ أَوْ نُظْلَمَ أَوْ نَجْهَلَ أَوْ يُجْهَلَ عَلَيْنَا

Bismillāhi tawakkaltu 'alallāhi. Allāhumma innā na'ūdhu bika min an nazilla aw nadilla aw nazlima aw nuzlama aw najhala aw yujhala 'alaynā.

In the name of Allāh, I place my trust in Allāh. O Allāh! We seek Your protection from slipping unintentionally or becoming misguided, or committing oppression or being oppressed, or acting ignorantly or being treated ignorantly. (Tirmidhī)

23.   When one boards any vehicle, one should read:

بِسْمِ اللهِ

Bismillāh

In the name of Allāh

When seated, one should read:

اَلْحَمْدُ لِلّهِ

Alhamdulillāh

All praise is due to Allāh

Thereafter one should read the following du'ā:

سُبْحَانَ الَّذِيْ سَخَّرَ لَنَا هَذَا وَمَا كُنَّا لَهُ مُقْرِنِيْنَ وَإِنَّا إِلَى رَبِّنَا لَمُنْقَلِبُوْنَ

Subhānalladhī sakh-khara lanā hādhā wa mā kunnā lahū muqrinīn wa
innā ilā rabbinā lamun-qalibūn.

*Purity belongs to Allāh, Who has subjected this conveyance for us and we
were not capable of controlling it and surely to our Sustainer we are to
return.*

Thereafter, one should read each of the following three times:

اَلْحَمْدُ لِلّٰهِ

Alhamdulillāh

All praise is due to Allāh

اَللّٰهُ اَكْبَرُ

Allāhu Akbar

Allāh is the greatest

Thereafter, one should recite the following du'ā:

سُبْحَانَكَ إِنِّيْ ظَلَمْتُ نَفْسِيْ فَاغْفِرْ لِيْ إِنَّهُ لاَ يَغْفِرُ الذُّنُوْبَ إِلَّا أَنْتَ

Subhānaka innī zalamtu nafsī faghfir lī innahū lā yaghfirudh dhunūba illā Anta.

Purity belongs to You. Surely I have wronged myself, so forgive me. Indeed none forgives sins besides You. (Abū Dāwūd)

Our Prophet ﷺ used to read the following du'ā as well:

اَللّٰهُمَّ إِنَّا نَسْأَلُكَ فِيْ سَفَرِنَا هٰذَا الْبِرَّ وَالتَّقْوٰى وَمِنَ الْعَمَلِ مَاتَرْضٰى اَللّٰهُمَّ هَوِّنْ عَلَيْنَا سَفَرَنَا هٰذَا وَاطْوِ عَنَّا بُعْدَهُ اَللّٰهُمَّ أَنْتَ الصَّاحِبُ فِي السَّفَرِ وَالْخَلِيْفَةُ فِي الْأَهْلِ اَللّٰهُمَّ إِنِّيْ أَعُوْذُ بِكَ مِنْ وَعْثَاءِ السَّفَرِ وَكَابَةِ الْمَنْظَرِ وَسُوْءِ الْمُنْقَلَبِ فِي الْمَالِ وَالْأَهْلِ

Allāhumma innā nas-aluka fī safarinā hādhal birra wat-taqwā wa minal 'amali mā tardā. Allāhumma hawwin 'alaynā safaranā hādhā watwi 'annā bu'dahu. Allāhumma Antas-Sāhibu fis-safari wal khalīfatu fil ahli. Allāhumma innī a'ūdhu bika min wa'thā'is-safari wa kābatil manzari wa sū'il munqalabi fil māli wal ahli.

O Allāh, we ask You on this journey of ours for goodness and piety and actions that please You. O Allāh, lighten this journey for us and make its distance easy for us. O Allāh, You are our Companion on this journey and the Guardian in our family. O Allāh, I seek refuge in You from this journey's hardship and from the distressful sights and from an evil turn (of circumstance) in my wealth and family (Muslim)

24.   When travelling on a ship, boat, canoe or other floating object one should read:

بِسْمِ اللهِ مَجْرَاهَا وَمُرْسَاهَا إِنَّ رَبِّيْ لَغَفُوْرٌ رَّحِيْمٌ

Bismillāhi majrēhā wa mursāhā inna rabbī laghafūrur-Rahīm.

In the name of Allāh is its sailing and anchoring. Surely, my Lord is Most Forgiving and Most Merciful. (Abū Dāwūd)

25. When one ascends or attempts to reach any height one should say:

اَللّٰهُ اَكْبَرُ

Allāhu Akbar

Allāh is the greatest

and when descending from any height one should say:

سُبْحَانَ الله

Subhān-Allāh

Purity belongs to Allāh (Bukhārī)

26. When one enters any village, town, settlement etc. one should read the following three times:

اَللّٰهُمَّ بَارِكْ لَنَا فِيْهَا

Allāhumma bārik lanā fīhā.

O Allāh, bless us in this (village, town etc.)

Thereafter, read the following duʿā:

اَللّٰهُمَّ ارْزُقْنَا جَنَاهَا وَ حَبِّبْنَا إِلٰى أَهْلِهَا وَ حَبِّبْ صَالِحِيْ أَهْلِهَا إِلَيْنَا

Allāhummar-zuqnā janāhā wa habbibnā ilā ahlihā wa habbib sālihī
ahlihā ilaynā.

*O Allāh, bless us with its fruits and create our love in the hearts of its
inhabitants and love for their pious in our hearts. (Tabarānī)*

27.   When returning from a journey one should read:

أَيِبُوْنَ تَائِبُوْنَ عَابِدُوْنَ لِرَبِّنَا حَامِدُوْنَ

Āibūna tāʾibūna ʿābidūna lirabbinā hāmidūn.

*We now return (from our journey) repenting (to Allāh), worshipping
(Him) and praising our Lord (Allāh). (Bukhārī, Muslim)*

28.   To perform two rakʿāt nafl (optional) salāh when one resumes
      his journey after halting at any location. *(Tabarānī, Bayhaqi)*
29.   To avoid returning home late from a lengthy journey. *(Bukhārī)*
30.   To bring back gifts for ones family members when returning
      from a journey. *(Dārul Qutnī, Kanzul ʿUmmāl)*
31.   To perform two rakʿāt salāh in the masjid as soon as one
      returns from the journey. *(Bukhārī)*
32.   To greet and embrace each other when returning from a
      journey. *(Abū Dāwūd)*

33. To invite family and friends to meals upon one's safe return from a journey. *(Bukhārī)*
34. When performing fardh salāh on a journey, to call out both the adhān and the iqāmat. *(Tirmidhī)*
35. Whilst on a journey, not to unnecessarily omit the sunnah mu'akkadah. *(Tirmidhī)*

Note: There are narrations which permit the omission of the sunnah salāh whilst travelling as well. Hence, the 'ulamā' explain that it all depends on the circumstances. If a person is in a hurry, he could omit the sunnah salāh and if not, he should read it.

Sunnats Regarding Hospitality towards Guests

Sayyidunā Abū Hurairah ﷺ narrates that the holy Prophet ﷺ said, "A person who believes in Allāh ﷻ and in the last day, should honour his guest." *(Bukhārī)*

1. To welcome the guest. *(Bukhārī)*
2. To fulfil the rights of the guest. *(Bukhārī)*
3. To personally entertain and serve the guest (like Sayyidunā Ibrāhīm عليه السلام did with his guests).
4. To bid farewell to the guest up to the door. *(Ibn Mājah)*
5. A guest should be entertained and shown hospitality for a period of three days. Beyond the three day period would be considered as charity. *(Bukhārī)*
6. Special meals and hospitality should be given for at least the first day. *(Bukhārī, Muslim)*
7. A guest should not inconvenience his host by overstaying. *(Bukhārī)*
8. The Prophet ﷺ has encouraged eating with the guest as the guest may feel uncomfortable eating alone. *(Ibn Hibbān)*
9. It is the responsibility of all the Muslims in general to take care of the visitor that comes at night. *(Abū Dāwūd)*

Note: This means that the passer-by who has not come as a guest to any specific person, but is to stay at any place due to nightfall is the responsibility of all the Muslims of that locality.

10.   The guest is a gift from Allāh ﷻ. When he comes, he brings his own sustenance, and when he leaves, the family that hosted him are forgiven. *(Kanzul 'Ummāl)*

11.   The noble habit of Sayyidunā Ibrāhīm عليه السلام was that he would never eat a meal without a guest. Sometimes he would walk for a long distance in search of a guest to join him in the meal. *(Ihyā'ul-Ulūm)*

12.   One will not have to answer for three types of food:
        a) That which is eaten at the time of iftār i.e. at the time of breaking the fast.
        b) That which is eaten at the time of suhūr i.e. pre-dawn (when beginning the fast)
        c) The food which is provided for one's Muslim guests. *(Daylamī)*

13.   One should not see the visitor off without arranging for his breakfast. *(Ibn Mājah)*

Note: This means that providing breakfast is also necessary upon the host who accommodates a guest for the night.

Sunnats Regarding Invitations

Sayyidunā Anas ﷺ reports that once a tailor prepared meals and invited the Prophet ﷺ. Sayyidunā Anas ﷺ says that he accompanied the Prophet ﷺ. *(Bukhārī)*

1.   The Prophet ﷺ encouraged accepting invitations even if it be partaking in a cheap dish.*(Bukhārī)*
2.   Whomsoever does not accept an invitation has disobeyed Allāh ﷻ and His Messenger ﷺ. *(Bukhārī)*

Note: The above hadīth applies only when the invitation conforms to the sunnah and it is based on sincerity. Where the objective is to show-off or boast or to receive something in return, or un-Islamic things are going to take place, then it would be permissible, and in certain cases obligatory to decline the invitation.

3.   The Prophet ﷺ said, "If you are invited to meals, accept the invitation. Thereafter, you have a choice of eating or not eating." *(Muslim)*
4.   If one cannot eat when invited (e.g. due to fasting) then one should at least make duʿā for the host. *(Muslim)*
5.   If the meal is not to one's liking, even then, not to leave but rather display patience. *(Ibn Hibbān)*
6.   If one receives two invitations for the same time, he should accept the invitation of the one whose door (home) is nearer

to his. If both of them live near his home, he should accept the invitation of the one who is the closer neighbour. If both are close neighbours, he should accept the invitation which he received first. *(Musnad Ahmad, Kanzul 'Ummāl)*

7.	The Prophet ﷺ has prohibited accepting the invitation of an open sinner. *(Majma'uz Zawāid)*

8.	The Prophet ﷺ has prohibited the eating of food of the proud people. *(Abū Dāwūd)*

Note: The hadīth prohibits eating the food of people who will boast about having fed a person, or who feed people in order to show off.

9.	Do not attend a function unless invited. The Prophet ﷺ said, "A person who attends a function without being invited attends as a thief and leaves as a looter." *(Abū Dāwūd)*

10.	One should not participate and return if one notices any un-Islamic practice. *(Bukhārī)*

11.	Imām Nawawī ﷺ writes that if the following occur, a person will be discouraged from attending;

- A person doubts if the food or the earning of the one inviting is halāl or not.
- If only the rich are invited.
- If open sinners and shameless people will be present in the gathering.
- If the invitation is for name and fame.
- It is a function where evil practices or un-Islamic acts will take place.

- Wine will be served (even if one is not going to drink).
- People will be made to sit on silk sheets.
- Unnecessary photography will take place.
- Gold or silver utensils will be used.

12. Feeding others is so superior in the eyes of Allāh ﷻ that He boasts in front of the angels about those who feed others. (*Targhīb*)

13. After partaking in the meal, to perform salāh and make du‘ā for blessings for the host. (*Bukhārī, Tahāwī*)

14. After eating iftār at a hosts' place, to supplicate for him in the following words:

$$ أَفْطَرَ عِنْدَكُمُ الصَّائِمُوْنَ وَأَكَلَ طَعَامَكُمُ الْأَبْرَارُ وَصَلَّتْ عَلَيْكُمُ الْمَلَائِكَةُ $$

Aftara ‘indakumus sāi’mūna wa akala ta‘āmakumul abrāru wa sallat ‘alaykumul malā’ikatu.

May the fasting (men) break their fast with you, and the pious eat your food, and the angels pray for blessings on you. (Ibn Mājah, Musnad Ahmad)

Also, the following du‘ā should be read at an invitation:

$$ اَللّٰهُمَّ أَطْعِمْ مَنْ أَطْعَمَنِيْ وَاسْقِ مَنْ سَقَانِيْ $$

Allāhumma at‘im man at‘amanī wasqi man saqānī.
O Allāh! Feed those who have fed me and quench those who have quenched me. (Muslim)

Sunnats Regarding Gifts

Sayyidah 'Ā'ishah 🙵 narrates that the Prophet 🙵 used to accept gifts and give the giver something in return as well. *(Bukhārī)*

1. Both to give and receive gifts is sunnah. *(Bukhārī)*
2. Giving and taking of gifts increases mutual love and removes malice. *(Tabarānī, Kanzul 'Ummāl)*
3. Any gifts received without asking or having any anticipation (secret desire) for it should be accepted and not returned. *(Bukhārī, Muslim)*

Note: The hadīth informs us that if any individual is given any gift without having yearned for it, or asking for it, he should accept it. What the hadīth prohibits is ishrāf - a condition wherein a person craves to receive something from another.

4. When giving gifts to one's children, it is preferable (mustahab) to give all the children equally. *(Bukhārī)*

Note: However, due to any virtue or other valid reason, it is permissible to give one child more than another, as Sayyidunā Abū Bakr as-Siddīq 🙵 gave more to Sayyidah 'Ā'ishah 🙵 than his other children. *(Tahāwī)*

5. Gifts should be given in secrecy. However, it is preferable for the recipient to mention the gift to others. *(Targhīb)*

6. The Prophet ﷺ has said that to take back a gift is like a dog licking its vomit. *(Bukhārī)*

7. To enquire from one bringing (anything) whether it is a gift or sadaqah. *(Bukhārī)*

8. The Prophet ﷺ used to give the sadaqah away to the deserving Sahābah ﷺ. However, the Prophet ﷺ ate from the gifts. *(Bukhārī)*

9. Exchanging of "food gifts" is a source of increase in one's sustenance. *(al-Jāmi' as-Saghīr)*

10. The Prophet ﷺ advised that one should add water to the gravy as this will enable one to help one's poor neighbours. *(Al-Adabul -Mufrad)*

11. A gift is a sustenance from Allāh ﷻ. Whoever is given a gift should accept it and replace it with a better one. *(Ibn Abid-Dunya)*

12. To give cash as a gift is also established from the sunnah. *(Shamā'il)*

13. It is permissible to send young children to pass gifts to others. *(Majma'uz Zawāid)*

14. The Prophet ﷺ accepted gifts from female Companions. *(Bukhārī)*

15. The Prophet ﷺ advised us to accept gifts even if it is low quality e.g. foot of a goat. *(Bukhārī)*

16. Not to accept any gift due to a valid shar'ī reason is allowed e.g. refusing food due to fasting. *(Tirmidhī, Muslim)*

17. To give the bride and groom gifts. *(Bukhārī)*

18. To give one's non-Muslim relatives gifts. *(Bukhārī)*

19. The neighbour that lives closer to one should be preferred when giving gifts. *(Bukhārī)*
20. The Prophet ﷺ advised not to accept the gift of the one to whom one had given a loan. *(Bukhārī)*

Note: To derive benefit after giving a loan is tantamount to ribā (interest) and is therefore prohibited. However, the scholars say that if the giving and receiving of gifts had been normal practice between them (prior to the loan) then it would not be prohibited.

21. The following gifts should not be refused:
    - Milk *(Tirmidhī)*
    - Pillow *(Tirmidhī)*
    - Perfume *(Bukhārī, Tirmidhī)*
    - Sweets *(Bazzār)*
    - Meat *(Ibn Mājah)*
    - Sweet-smelling flowers *(Tirmidhī)*
    - Oil *(Shamā'il)*

22. The Prophet ﷺ had said, "Whosoever does any kindness to you, repay it with another, and if you are incapable of doing that, then make duʿā for the person." *(Majmaʿuz Zawāid)*
23. The one who has said 'جَزَاكَ اللهُ خَيْرًا' (May Allāh ﷻ grant you the best reward) to the one who has given a gift has fully praised him. *(Musannaf Abdur Razzāq, Ibn Hibbān)*
24. It is preferable to distribute the gift given in a gathering amongst those present. *(Tirmidhī, Hākim)*

Note: This refers to food items only.

25. A person who accepts a gift from the one for whom he interceded has entered the doors of ribā (interest). *(Abū Dāwūd)*

26. The Prophet ﷺ prohibited those in positions of authority from accepting gifts. *(Bukhārī, Abū Dāwūd)*

Note: Such individuals are given gifts usually only due to their positions and hence, bribes.

Imām Bukhārī ﷺ has recorded the statement of 'Umar ibn 'Abdul 'Azīz ﷺ that he said, "Gifts were genuinely gifts in the era of the Prophet ﷺ, but these days they are nothing more than bribes." *(Bukhārī)*

Sunnats Regarding Majālis (Gatherings)

1.   To attend the gathering of righteous people. *(Bukhārī)*
2.   To abstain from un-Islamic gatherings. *(Tirmidhī)*
3.   To refrain from gathering and sitting on public paths. *(Bukhārī)*
4.   To stay away from holding non-beneficial gatherings and socialising after 'Ishā Salāh. *(Bukhārī)*

Note: A person should immediately go to sleep after 'Ishā or engage in righteous deeds.

5.   To greet when attending the gathering. *(Abū Dāwūd)*
6.   To create space for the one joining the gathering. *(Qur'ān - 58:11)*
7.   To remove the shoes when sitting in the gathering. *(Abū Dāwūd)*
8.   To sit down wherever you find any space. *(Tabarāni, Bayhaqi)*
9.   Not to sit between two people without their permission. *(Abū Dāwūd)*
10. To refrain from sitting in the middle of the gathering or the study circles. *(Abū Dāwūd)*
11. The Prophet ﷺ has prohibited to remove any person from his seat and to sit in his place. *(Bukhārī, Muslim)*
12. To remember Allāh ﷻ in every gathering and in every majlis. *(Abū Dāwūd)*

13. To focus fully and attentively towards the person who is speaking. *(Shamā'il)*
14. If two people are sitting and discussing, then not to join in that gathering but with their permission. *(Bukhārī)*
15. If there are three people, then two people should not engage in conversation leaving the third person. *(Bukhārī)*

Note: This will include speaking in a foreign language which the other person does not understand.

16. To avoid excessive laughter and jokes. *(Ibn Mājah)*
17. To welcome and smile at the attendees of the gathering. *(Muslim)*
18. To recite the following du'ā before standing up from any gathering:

سُبْحَانَكَ اَللّٰهُمَّ وَبِحَمْدِكَ أَشْهَدُ أَنْ لَّا إِلٰهَ إِلَّا أَنْتَ أَسْتَغْفِرُكَ وَأَتُوْبُ إِلَيْكَ

Subhānaka, Allāhumma wa bihamdika ash-hadu al-lā ilāha illā Anta. Astaghfiruka wa atūbu ilayka.

Exalted are You. O Allāh, by Your praise; I bear witness that there is no god but You. I seek forgiveness from You and I repent to You.

Whoever recites this du'ā will have all the sins committed by him in the gathering forgiven. *(Tirmidhī)*

Sunnats Regarding Visiting the Sick

Sayyidunā 'Alī ﷺ states that he heard the Prophet ﷺ say, "When a Muslim visits a sick Muslim at dawn, seventy thousand angels keep on praying for him till dusk. If he visits him in the evening, seventy thousand angels keep on praying for him till the morning; and he will have (his share of) reaped fruits in Jannah." *(Tirmidhī)*

1. To visit the sick with the intention of thawāb (reward) and to gain Allāh's ﷺ pleasure. *(Muslim)*
2. To visit the sick even if it may be a small child. *(Bukhārī)*
3. To visit the sick even if it may be a non-Muslim and to invite them to Islām. *(Bukhārī)*
4. To visit the sick by foot (if possible).
5. To enquire from the family regarding the sick person. *(Bukhārī)*
6. One must take good care of the sick in their community. *(Bukhārī)*
7. To sit by the head side of the sick. *(Bukhārī)*
8. When visiting the sick, one should first greet the patient and then enquire about his health. *(Tirmidhī)*
9. The Prophet ﷺ used to place his hand on the patient's head when visiting him. *(Bukhārī)*
10. One should always encourage the sick person and be careful not to speak of things that may cause despair or loss of hope. *(Tirmidhī, Ibn Mājah)*
11. One should not visit the sick for too long (to overstay such that the sick will be inconvenienced). *(Bayhaqi)*

12.   To request the patient to make du'ā as his du'ās are accepted.

Sayyidunā 'Umar al-Fārūq ﷺ states that the Prophet ﷺ said to me, "When you visit a sick person, request him to pray for you because his supplication for you is like that of the angels." *(Ibn Mājah)*

13.   One should, as far as possible, give the patient whatever he asks for as long as the item or food requested is not harmful (to the patient). *(Ibn Mājah)*

14.   To stop the sick from desiring death. *(Hākim)*

15.   One should read the following du'ā when visiting the ill:

$$\text{لَا بَأْسَ طَهُوْرٌ إِنْ شَاءَ اللهُ}$$

Lā ba'sa tahūrun in shā' Allāh.

No need to worry. It (this illness) is a purifier (of sins), Allāh willing.
(Bukhārī)

16.   Furthermore, when visiting the ill, a person should read the following du'ā seven times:

$$\text{أَسْأَلُ اللهَ الْعَظِيْمَ رَبَّ الْعَرْشِ الْعَظِيْمِ أَنْ يَّشْفِيَكَ}$$

As'alullāh hal-'Azīma Rabbal 'arshil 'azīmi an yashfiyaka.

I ask Allāh the Great Who is the Sustainer of the Great Throne to give you shifā (cure). (Abū Dāwūd)

Benefit: The Prophet ﷺ said that whenever a Muslim visits a Muslim patient and reads the above du'ā seven times, the patient will definitely recover from his illness except such illness which will result in death. *(Abū Dāwūd)*

17. Whoever reads the following du'ā upon seeing another afflicted with sickness or difficulty shall himself be saved from it (inshā'Allāh):

اَلْحَمْدُ لِلّٰهِ الَّذِيْ عَافَانِيْ مِمَّا ابْتَلَاكَ بِهٖ وَفَضَّلَنِيْ عَلٰى كَثِيْرٍ مِّمَّنْ خَلَقَ تَفْضِيْلًا

Alhamdulillāh hilladhī 'āfānī mimmab-talāka bihī wa faddalanī 'alā kathīrim-mimman khalaqa tafdīlā.

All praise is due to Allāh Who has saved me from that which He afflicted you and gave me excellence over most of whom He created. (Tirmidhī)

Note: It is advisable to read this du'ā inaudibly or at a distance from the patient.

18. When feeling pain in the body, one should place the right hand on the affected area and recite Bismillāh three times and thereafter recite the following du'ā seven times:

أَعُوْذُ بِعِزَّةِ اللّٰهِ وَقُدْرَتِهٖ مِنْ شَرِّ مَا أَجِدُ وَأُحَاذِرُ

A'ūdhu bi'izzatil-lāhi wa qudratihī min sharri mā ajidu wa uhādhir.

I seek refuge in the might and power of Allāh from the evil of the pain I feel and fear. (Muslim, Muwatta Mālik)

19. Sayyidah 'Ā'ishah ﷺ reports that whenever anyone fell sick, the Prophet ﷺ used to pass his hands over his face and chest and recite the following du'ā:

اَللّٰهُمَّ رَبَّ النَّاسِ أَذْهِبِ الْبَأْسَ اِشْفِ أَنْتَ الشَّافِي لَا شِفَاءَ إِلَّا شِفَاؤُكَ شِفَاءٌ لَّا يُغَادِرُ سَقَمًا

Allāhumma Rabban-nāsi, adh-hibil ba'sa ishfi Antash-Shāfi. Lā shifā'a illā shifā'uka shifā'un lā yughādiru saqaman.

O Allāh, Lord of mankind, remove all harm, cure as You are the One Who cures. There is no cure but Your cure; a cure that leaves no illness.
(Bukhārī, Muslim)

20. The following du'ā should be read after the morning and evening prayers for protection from all evils:

بِسْمِ اللهِ الَّذِيْ لَا يَضُرُّ مَعَ اسْمِهِ شَيْءٌ فِي الْأَرْضِ وَلَا فِي السَّمَاءِ وَهُوَ السَّمِيْعُ الْعَلِيْمُ

Bismillāh hilladhī lā yadurru ma'a ismihī shay-un fil ardi wa lā fis-samā'i wa Huwas-Samī'ul 'Alīm.

In the name of Allāh by Whose name nothing on earth and nothing in heaven can cause harm. He is the All-Hearing, the All-Knowing.

Benefit: Whoever reads this duʿā thrice in the morning or evening, nothing will harm him till the evening or morning. *(Tirmidhī)*

Sunnats Regarding Death

Etiquettes Before Death

1. For the dying person to have good thoughts and opinions regarding Allāh ﷻ. *(Muslim)*

2. To make the dying person wear clean or new clothes if possible. *(Abū Dāwūd)*

3. To recite Sūrah Yāsīn next to the dying person. *(Bayhaqi)*

Benefit: Reciting Sūrah Yāsīn shall lessen the pangs of death.

4. The face of the dying person should be turned towards the qiblah and the person suffering the throes of death should read:

اَللّٰهُمَّ اغْفِرْ لِيْ وَارْحَمْنِيْ وَأَلْحِقْنِيْ بِالرَّفِيْقِ الْأَعْلٰى

Allāhummagh-firlī war-hamnī wa alhiqnī birrafiqil-a'lā

O Allāh, forgive me and be merciful to me and join me with the Companion of the loftiest rank.

اَللّٰهُمَّ أَعِنِّيْ عَلٰى غَمَرَاتِ الْمَوْتِ وَسَكَرَاتِ الْمَوْتِ

Allāhumma a'innī 'alā ghamarātil mawti wa sakarātil mawti.

O Allāh! Help me at this moment of the agony of death.

5. To do *talqīn i.e.* recall the dying person with Lā ilāha illallāh. (*Muslim*)

Note: The people around must do the *talqīn* until the dying person recites the kalimah. *Talqīn* thereafter is not essential but if the dying person talks of worldly matters then the *talqīn* should be repeated.

Etiquettes After Death

1. The family and relatives of the deceased should read the following du'ā upon the confirmation of death:

إِنَّا لِلّٰهِ وَإِنَّا إِلَيْهِ رَاجِعُوْنَ اَللّٰهُمَّ أُجُرْنِيْ فِيْ مُصِيْبَتِيْ وَأَخْلِفْ لِيْ خَيْرًا مِّنْهَا

Innā lillāhi wa innā ilayhi rāji'ūn. Allāhumma' jurnī fi musībatī wa akhlif lī khayran minhā.

To Allāh we belong and to Him is our return. O Allāh! Repay me for what has befallen me and compensate me with what is better. (*Muslim*)

2. To endure the tragedy and shock with patience. (*Bukhārī*)
3. To submit to the decree of Allāh ﷻ and abstain from complaining. (*Bukhārī*)
4. To close the eyes of the deceased. (*Ibn Mājah*)
5. To mention good things in front of the deceased. (*Muslim*)

6. To mention the good qualities and points of the deceased. (*Abū Dāwūd*)
7. To send food to the deceased's house. (*Abū Dāwūd*)
8. To shed tears without wailing and complaining is permissible and only natural. (*Bukhārī*)
9. It is permissible to kiss the deceased whether on the face or the forehead. (*Ibn Mājah, Abū Dāwūd*)

Sunnats Regarding Ghusl and Shrouding

1. To wash the dead body an odd number of times (preferably three times). (*Bukhārī*)
2. To commence with the wudhū for the deceased. (*Bukhārī*)
3. To start from the right-hand side. (*Bukhārī*)
4. Not to expose any of the faults or sins of the deceased. (*Tabarānī*)

Note: If the deceased was an open sinner and the exposure would be a lesson for the general public, then it would be permissible.

5. To use sidr (fragrant leaf) or camphor fragrance during the ghusl. (*Bukhārī*)
6. To use white clothes for shrouding the deceased. (*Abū Dāwūd*)

Note: Male deceased should be shrouded in three cloths and women in five cloths.

Sunnats Regarding Janāzah

1. To hasten with the janāzah. *(Bukhārī)*
2. To walk behind the janāzah. *(Bukhārī)*
3. To walk with the coffin if possible towards the graveyard. *(Tirmidhī)*
4. For the men only to lift the janāzah (coffin). *(Bukhārī)*
5. Not to sit until the janāzah has not been put down. *(Muslim)*
6. To briefly address the audience at the funeral prayer. *(Bukhārī)*
7. For the imām to stand in parallel to the chest of the deceased. *(Bukhārī)*
8. To arrange odd number of rows in the funeral prayer. *(Abū Dāwūd)*
5. To make sincere du'ā for the deceased. *(Abū Dāwūd)*

Sunnats Regarding Burial

1. To attend the janāzah and the burial. *(Bukhārī)*
2. To avoid burial in the night. *(Ibn Mājah)*
3. To commence filling the grave from the head-side. *(Ibn Mājah)*
4. To throw three handfuls of earth in the grave. To recite the following du'ā:

مِنْهَا خَلَقْنَاكُمْ وَفِيْهَا نُعِيْدُكُمْ وَمِنْهَا نُخْرِجُكُمْ تَارَةً أُخْرٰى
بِسْمِ اللّٰهِ وَفِيْ سَبِيْلِ اللّٰهِ وَعَلٰى مِلَّةِ رَسُوْلِ اللّٰهِ

Min hā khalaqnākum wa fīhā nu'īdukum wa minhā nukhrijukum tāratan ukhrā. Bismillāhi wa fī sabī-lillāhi wa 'alā millati rasūlillāhi.

From it (the earth) did We create you and into it shall We return you and from it shall We bring you out once again. In the name of Allāh and in the path of Allāh and upon the dīn of the Messenger of Allāh. (Ibn Mājah)

5. To sprinkle water over the grave after the burial. *(Bayhaqi, Tabarāni)*
6. To remain by the grave for a short while after the burial. *(Muslim)*
7. To pray and ask for forgiveness on behalf of the deceased after the burial. *(Abū Dāwūd)*
8. To recite Sūrah Fātihah and the beginning verses of Sūrah Baqarah (until "Muflihūn") at the head-side and the

concluding verses of Sūrah Baqarah (starting from "Āmanar-Rasūlu" until the end) at the leg-side of the deceased. *(Tabarāni)*

Sunnats Regarding the Graveyard

1. To recite the following du'ā when visiting the graveyard:

اَلسَّلَامُ عَلَيْكُمْ يَا أَهْلَ الْقُبُوْرِ يَغْفِرُ اللّٰهُ لَنَا وَلَكُمْ أَنْتُمْ سَلَفُنَا وَنَحْنُ بِالْأَثَرِ

Assalāmu 'alaykum yā ahlal qubūr. Yaghfirullāhu lanā wa lakum, antum salafunā wa nahnu bil athar.

Peace be upon you, O dwellers of these graves. May Allāh forgive you and us. You have preceded us and we are following your trail. (Tirmidhī)

One can recite the following du'ā as well:

اَلسَّلَامُ عَلَيْكُمْ أَهْلَ الدِّيَارِ مِنَ الْمُؤْمِنِيْنَ وَالْمُسْلِمِيْنَ، وَإِنَّا إِنْ شَاءَ اللّٰهُ لَلَاحِقُوْنَ، أَسْأَلُ اللّٰهَ لَنَا وَلَكُمُ الْعَافِيَةَ

Assalāmu 'alaykum ahl-ad-diyāri minal-mu'minīna wal-muslimīna, wa innā inshā'-Allāhu la-lāhiqūna, nas'alullāha lanā wa-lakumul-āfiyah

Peace be upon you all, O inhabitants of the dwellings (i.e. the graves), amongst the believers and the Muslims. Indeed we are, Allāh willing, soon to follow (to die also), we ask Allāh for well-being for us and for you." (Muslim)

3. To carry out charitable deeds for the deceased. *(Ibn Mājah)*

4. To avoid walking over the graves. *(Muslim)*
5. Not to sit upon the graves. *(Muslim)*
6. It is prohibited to build on the graves. *(Muslim)*
7. It is harām to read salāh towards the grave. *(Muslim)*

Sunnats Regarding Ta'ziyat (Condolence)

Ta'ziyat refers to sympathising with the bereaved. The Prophet ﷺ has said, "He who consoles the one in distress shall be rewarded as much as the bereaved." *(Tirmidhī)*

Note: One should keep in mind the following points during ta'ziyat:

- One should be most humble.
- Express his grief.
- Speak less about worldly affairs.
- Should not joke or laugh
- Mention the good acts and deeds of the deceased and refrain from the ill ones.

1. To express sympathy with a deceased's family and encourage them to show patience and accept the will of Allāh ﷻ. *(Tirmidhī)*
2. To express condolences with masnūn du'ās mentioned in the

ahādīth.

إِنَّ لِلّٰهِ مَا أَخَذَ وَلَهُ مَا أَعْطَى وَكُلُّ شَيْءٍ عِنْدَهُ بِأَجَلٍ مُّسَمًّى فَلْتَصْبِرْ وَلْتَحْتَسِبْ

Innā lillāhi mā akhadha, wa lahū mā a'tā wa kullu shay-in 'indahū bi ajalim musamman. Fal tasbir wal tahtasib.

Indeed Allāh takes what is His, and what He gives is His, and for all things He has appointed a time. So have patience and hope for reward.
(Bukhārī)

أَعْظَمَ اللّٰهُ أَجْرَكُمْ وَغَفَرَ اللّٰهُ لِصَاحِبِكُمْ

A'dhamallāhu ajrakum wa ghafarallāhu lisāhibikum.

Allāh increase your reward and Allāh forgive your companion. (Musannaf 'Abdur-Razzāq)

3. It is not proper for a Muslim to mourn for a dead person for more than three days. However, for a widow the mourning period is four months and ten days. *(Bukhārī)*

Sunnats When a Child is Born

The Prophet ﷺ said, "On the Day of Resurrection, you will be called by your names and by your father's names, so give yourselves good names." *(Abū Dāwūd)*

1. To name the children after the names of prophets. *(Musannaf)*
2. To give the new born an appropriate name on the seventh day. *(Tirmidhī, Abū Dāwūd)*
3. The first words to reach the child's ears should be the message of the greatness and Oneness of Allāh ﷻ and the prophethood of Rasūlullāh ﷺ. This is done by giving adhān near the right ear and iqāmat close to the left ear of the new born. *(Tirmidhī)*

Note: This noble act should be preferably done by a scholar or pious elder. If such a person is not immediately available then any Muslim male may perform this sunnah.

4. To perform tahnīk. *(Muslim)*

Note: Tahnīk is the placing of a date, softened by chewing, on the tongue of the new born. The act of tahnīk should be done by an 'ālim or a pious elder of the family preferably. If such a person is not available then any Muslim may perform this.

5. To carry out 'aqīqah on the seventh day. *(Tirmidhī)*

Note: 'Aqīqah is a form of sadaqah (charity) whereby the child is safeguarded against misfortune. Preferably two sheep or alternatively two goats are offered in the case of a male and one goat or one sheep suffices in the case of a female. If, for some reason, 'aqīqah was not made on the seventh day, then it can be done on the fourteenth, the twenty-first, twenty-eighth (or any other day in multiples of seven thereafter). The sooner 'aqīqah is performed, the better.

6. To remove the baby's hair on the seventh day after birth. Silver equivalent to the weight of the removed hair may be given as charity to the poor, otherwise its equivalent value in money will suffice. (*Abū Dāwūd, Tirmidhī*)

Note: After the birth, the placenta and novel cord should be buried with due care since they are parts of the human body. Upon birth, the new born should be given a proper ghusl (bath).

7. To carry out the circumcision for the male at an early age. (*Tirmidhī*)
8. To teach children the kalimah (Lā ilāha illallāhu Muhammadur Rasūlullāh) when they start to speak. (*Kanzul 'Ummāl*)
9. To teach good etiquettes and conduct from an early age. (*Bukhārī*)

Benefit: 'Amr ibn Abī Salamah ﷺ narrates, "I was a boy under the care of the Messenger of Allāh ﷺ and as my hand used to wander around in the dish, he said to me once, 'Mention Allāh's name (i.e., say Bismillāh), eat with your right hand and eat from what is in front of you.'" *(Bukhārī, Muslim)*

10. To instruct salāh to the children when they are seven years of age and to discipline them (if they do not perform salāh) when they are ten years of age. *(Abū Dāwūd)*

11. To separate the bedding of the children when the child attains ten years of age. *(Abū Dāwūd, Tirmidhī)*

Sunnats Regarding the Recitation of the Qur'ān

The Prophet ﷺ has said, "The best amongst you are those who have learnt the holy Qur'ān and teach it to others." *(Bukhārī)*

1. To recite the Qur'ān for the pleasure of Allāh ﷻ. *(Nasa'i)*
2. To recite the Qur'ān in the state of wudhū. *(Ihyā'ul-'Ulūm, Tahāwi)*
3. To recite the Qur'ān with tajwīd (correct pronounciation). *(Sūrah Muzzammil)*
4. To recite with a sweet voice and not a singing tone. *(Abū Dāwūd)*
5. To ponder and contemplate over the verses of the Qur'ān. *(Sūrah Muhammad)*
6. To refrain from talking whilst reciting the Qur'ān. *(Bukhārī)*
7. To weep when reading verses of fear and Jahannam and to express joy when reading verses of Jannah and glad tidings. *(Muslim)*

Benefits: There is so much reward in reciting and learning the holy Qur'ān. The holy Prophet ﷺ said, "Whoever recites one letter from the holy Qur'ān, will get one good deed in reward and this one good deed will be equal to ten good deeds. I do not say that Alif, Lām, Mīm is a letter but Alif is a letter, Lām is a letter and Mīm is a letter (i.e. it is equal to three letters, thus attaining thirty rewards)." *(Tirmidhī)*

As Muslims we should have a strong connection with the holy Qur'ān. The holy Prophet ﷺ has said, "One whose heart does not contain anything from the holy Qur'ān is like a deserted house." *(Tirmidhī)*

Some of the Ādāb of Reciting the Holy Qur'ān

1. The reciter of the holy Qur'ān should perform wudhū.
2. To sit with respect when reciting the holy Qur'ān.
3. To place the holy Qur'ān on a stand or something high.
4. To commence the recitation with ta'awwudh (A'ūdhu billāhi minash-Shaytānir rajīm) and tasmiyah (Bismillāhir-Rahmānir-Rahīm).
5. Not to indulge in talking whilst reciting the holy Qur'ān.
6. The intention whilst reciting the Qur'ān should be to gain the pleasure of Allāh ﷻ.
7. The voice should not be raised to such an extent where a person's recitation will disturb others who are also engaged in some form of worship.
8. The reciter of the holy Qur'ān should sit in a dignified position facing the qiblah.

Foods Eaten by Our Prophet ﷺ

Below is a list of those foods which our Prophet ﷺ mentioned of their benefits or he himself praised and liked.

Those foods which our Prophet ﷺ ate, whether once in his blessed lifetime or as a habit are as follows.

- Meat; such as a camel, cow, sheep, goat, chicken, rabbit, buck (male deer), halāl birds and fish (whether dried in the sun or cooked with or without gravy).
- Dates of all types, including ripe and dry etc.
- Barely and wheat bread
- Vinegar
- Tharīd - bread (or roti) soaked in gravy with few pieces of meat
- Olive oil, ghee and butter
- Cheese
- Black pepper and other spices
- Beetroot, marrow, musk melon and cucumber
- Honey
- Fruits such as grapes, figs, melon and pomegranate.
- Pumpkin

1. The Prophet ﷺ said, "Meat is the most superior of dishes in this world and the Hereafter." *(Ibn Mājah)*

Note: Ibnul-Qayyim ﷺ writes that meat should not be consumed on a daily basis. Eating meat consecutively hardens the heart. Hence, the Prophet ﷺ did not eat meat continuously.

2. Sayyidunā Abū Mūsā al-Ash'ari ﷺ reports that he saw the Prophet ﷺ eating chicken. *(Bukhārī)*

3. Sayyidah 'Ā'ishah ﷺ narrates that the Prophet ﷺ loved sweetmeats and honey. *(Bukhārī)*

4. The Prophet ﷺ said, "Vinegar is such a good curry." *(Tirmidhī)*

5. The Prophet ﷺ loved milk. Whenever the Prophet ﷺ was offered milk, he used to say, "Barakah, Barakah" (blessings). *(Ibn Mājah)*

6. The Prophet ﷺ has said, "Nothing can substitute for solids and liquids at once except milk." *(Ibn Mājah)*

7. Sayyidunā Anas ﷺ relates that the Prophet ﷺ used to eat pumpkin excessively and he used to say that it sharpens the mind and increases intelligence. *(Bayhaqi)*

8. Sayyidah 'Ā'ishah ﷺ relates that sometimes couple of months used to pass and no fire would be lit in the Prophet's ﷺ house (as there was nothing to be cooked). She says that they used to survive on dates and water. *(Bukhārī)*

9. Sayyidunā 'Umar ﷺ relates that the Prophet ﷺ said, "Season (your food) with olive oil and anoint yourselves with it, for it comes from a blessed tree." *(Ibn Mājah)*

10. Sayyidunā 'Alī ﷺ narrates that the Prophet ﷺ said that we should eat pomegranate as it cleanses the stomach." *(Musnad Ahmad, Majma')*

11. The Prophet ﷺ enjoyed figs and said that it is the most beneficial for the treatment of piles. *(Ibnus Sunni)*

12. Sayyidunā Anas ibn Mālik ؓ narrates that he saw the Prophet ﷺ eating dates and musk melon together. *(Shamā'il)*

Note: The reason for eating dates with musk melon was because the musk melon lacked sweetness. A more suitable reason is that eating a hot and a cold fruit together maintains the balance in the body. *(Khasā'il)*

13. Sayyidunā 'Abdullāh ibn Ja'far ؓ narrates that the Prophet ﷺ would eat dates and cucumber together. *(Shamā'il)*

Note: This as mentioned above, could be to create a balance and also to sweeten the taste of the cucumbers. *(Khasā'il)*

14. Amongst the parts of the animal, the Prophet ﷺ liked the shoulder. *(Bukhārī)*

15. The Prophet ﷺ praised tharīd. *(Bukhārī)*

Sayyidunā 'Abdullāh ibn 'Abbās ؓ narrates that tharīd was the most beloved of all foods to the Prophet ﷺ.

Note: Tharīd is a dish where pieces of bread are soaked in meat that has been cooked with gravy. This food is easily digested and provides strength to the body.

Physical Description of Our Beloved Prophet ﷺ

Note: It is impossible to capture the true beauty and elegance of our beloved Prophet ﷺ. Nonetheless, some aḥādīth are enlisted from the books of Shamā'il to give us a glimpse of his extraordinary physical features.

1. Sayyidunā Abū Hurairah ؓ narrates, "I have never seen anyone more beautiful that the Prophet ﷺ. The Prophet's ﷺ noble face shone so brightly that it seemed as if the sun was radiating from his face." *(Ibn Sa'd)*
2. Sayyidunā 'Alī ؓ used to say, "The Messenger of Allāh ﷺ was neither very tall nor short, but of medium stature among people.

His hair was neither very curly nor very straight, but had a slight wave in it.

He did not have a big body nor a round face, nor a fully elongated face, but in between the two.

The complexion of Rasūlullāh ﷺ was white with redness in it.

The blessed eyes of Rasūlullāh ﷺ were extremely black. His eyelashes were long.

The joints of the body (i.e. elbows and knees etc.) were large. Likewise the portion between the two shoulders was broad and fully fleshed.

There was no hair (more than normal) on his body. (Some people have excessive hair on their body. Rasūlullāh ﷺ did not have hair on the parts of his body besides places like the arms and legs etc.)

He had a thin line of hair running from his chest to the navel.

The hands and feet of Rasūlullāh ﷺ were fully fleshed.

When he walked, he lifted his legs with vigour, as if he were descending to a low-lying place.

When he addressed a person, he turned his whole body towards that person (he did not only turn his face towards the person addressed, as this is considered impolite and sometimes, it even denotes pride).

Rasūlullāh ﷺ faced the person he spoke to, with his chest and body.

The seal of prophethood was situated between his shoulders.

He was the last of all prophets.

He was the most generous and the most truthful.
He was the most kind-hearted and came from the most noble family.

Any person who saw him suddenly would become awe-inspired.

Rasūlullāh ﷺ had such a great personality and dignity, that the person who saw him for the first time, because of his awe-inspiring personality, would be overcome with a feeling of profound respect.

Anyone who came in close contact with him, and knew his excellent character was overwhelmed with the love of his excellent attributes.

Anyone who described his noble features can only say, 'I have not seen anyone like Rasūlullāh ﷺ, neither before or after him.'" *(Shamā'il Tirmidhī)*

Quranic Wonders

The science of Tafsīr in itself is very vast, hence the compilation of these specific verses provides the reader with a simple and brief commentary. It is aimed to equip the reader with a small glimpse of the profound beauty of the Holy Qur'ān so that they can gain the passion to study further in depth. It is hoped that this will become a means of encouragement to increase the zeal and enthusiasm to recite and inculcate the teachings of the Holy Qur'ān into our daily lives. **UK RRP:£5:00**

Protection in the Grave

Sūrah Al-Mulk encapsulates the purpose of our creation - that we were created to live a life of obedience to our Lord and Creator. This can only be made to manifest through our good deeds which we perform solely for the sake of Allāh 🕮, in order to seek His pleasure. The Holy Prophet 🕮 told his Ummah to recite this Sūrah every night and learn this Sūrah by heart. The importance of this Sūrah is stressed due to the fact that the Holy Prophet 🕮 never slept until he had finished reciting this Sūrah. **UK RRP:£4:00**

Protection from Black Magic

These last ten Sūrahs are not only distinct in their meanings and message which will be discussed in this book, but also the fact that every Muslim should have these Sūrahs committed to memory as a minimum requirement in seeking refuge in Allāh 🕮 from all harm and evil, and every imperfection as well as seeking solace and peace in understanding His might and attributes. **UK RRP:£5:00**

Nurturing Children in Islam

Bringing up children has never been an easy duty. The challenges do not get easier as they get older either. Our emotions and other priorities sometimes hinder in nurturing our children, and as such, we fail to assist our children in reaching their potential by continually stumbling over our own perception of what we consider as ideal children. Our duty to our children is not without accountability. Our neglect and lack of interest in our children will be held to task. **UK RRP:£5:00**

Best of Stories

Sūrah Yūsuf is more than just a story of one of our beloved Prophets ﷺ there is much wisdom and lessons to be learnt and understood. All the knowledge comes from our honourable Shaykh, inspiration and Ustādh Shaykh Mufti Saiful Islām Sāhib. May Allāh ﷻ shower Mufti Sāhib with mercy and accept the day in, day out effort he carries out in the work of Dīn. **UK RRP:£4:00**

Call of Nuh

For 950 years, Sayyidunā Nūh ﷺ persevered night and day in continuous succession in preaching the message; unwavering and relentless in his mission. Not once did he feel that his calling was in vain. He stood firm and resolute in continuing with the mission that he was sent with, in proclaiming the message of the oneness of Allāh ﷻ; year after year, decade upon decade, century after century, but this failed to convince the people of the truth. **UK RRP:£4:00**

A Glimpse of Paradise

Time is the true wealth we have at our disposal though it cannot be amassed. The only way we can utilise it to our advantage is when we do righteous deeds and actions; for this will act in our favour in the Ākhirah (Hereafter). These moments will be preserved in exchange for moments of greater happiness and bliss in the next life. Therefore, we need to perform righteous deeds and actions in the short duration of time we have at our disposal in this temporary worldly life.

UK RRP:£4:00

Six Qualities of a Believer

Respected readers, do you want to be successful in this life and the Hereafter? The fact that you have prompted yourself to pick up this book and read, is an indication that the answer is *yes*. Or perhaps, you were not aware of the contents and purpose of this book and hence, eternal success wasn't the first thing on your mind. Nonetheless, it is easy to turn your attention towards this objective right now. **UK RRP:£2:00**

Ready for Judgement Day?

For those that doubt the Day of Resurrection, Allāh ﷻ is reaffirming that there is no scope for uncertainty; this day is indisputable and will surely occur. The day when the truth will be laid out bare and everything will be exposed, there will be no place to flee or escape to. Regretting that day will be of no avail; excuses will fail to safeguard or shelter a person from breaking free and escaping judgement. **UK RRP:£4:00**

Flee Towards Allāh ﷻ

Sūrah Al-Ma'ārij begins by addressing the disbelievers who used to mock the Holy Prophet ﷺ about the Day of Judgement. In this Surah, Allāh ﷻ severely reproaches those who deny it assuming that there is only one life; the life of this world. The Sūrah manifests its horrors and catastrophic scenes that the entire creation shall witness on that very day. Mankind will then realise that on this horrific day, they will be judged by their own actions. **UK RRP:£4:00**

Lanterns of Knowledge

Once the commentary of Kitābul 'Ilm in Bukhāri was completed, we realised that this chapter is an entire topic in itself due to its fascinating and insightful perspective on knowledge. When compiling this commentary, there were many beautiful reminders as well as points of guidance for everyone's personal life as well as their lifelong quest for knowledge. Therefore, the commentary of this chapter alone would be beneficial for all seekers of knowledge and the idea of publishing it as a separate book came to mind. **UK RRP:£10:00**

TIME IS RUNNING OUT

As the title suggests, as each day passes, we come closer to our death. Life is too short to be treated as an amusement and for the fulfillment of one's lust. The Day of Judgement is inevitable where we all must one day stand in front of the Lord of the Worlds to give an account of our deeds. These six Sūrahs explain the horrors and terrifying moments of Judgement Day and the inevitable standing before the Lord. We must therefore prepare for the Hereafter by realizing our purpose in life; to worship Allāh ﷻ Alone and reduce our worldly expectations. **UK RRP:£4:00**

Living Islām in Modern Times

This book is a compilation of various articles written by Shaykh Dr Rafāqat Rashīd Sāhib in the popular Al-Mu'min Magazine. Considering the great benefit these articles will bring to the Ummah, Mufti Saiful Islām Sāhib decided to edit and transform them into a book format, making the content easily accessible for readers.

UK RRP:£4:00

A CLEAR VICTORY

This book "A Clear Victory" is an enlightening commentary of Sūrah Al-Fath. It is cited in Sahīh Al-Bukhārī regarding the virtue of this Sūrah that Sayyidunā Umar Ibn Al-Khattāb ﷺ reported that the Messenger of Allāh ﷺ said: "This night a Sūrah was sent down to me that is more beloved to me than all what the sun shines over," then he read, "*We have indeed accorded a triumph to you, a manifest triumph, indeed*". **UK RRP:£5:00**